MW01503248

The Examined Life

Our Spiritual Journey

Selected "On Religion" Columns

written by

Sally Santana

for

The Kitsap Sun

1999 through 2005

Sophia Publishing

Blessings to you on your spiritual journey —
Sally Santana

First Edition
© 2006 by Sally Santana, Sophia Publishing.

All rights reserved. No part of this book shall be reproduced
in any form by any means, electronic or mechanical,
including photocopying, recording, or other means without
prior written permission of the publisher.

ISBN: 0-9788412-0-4 Soft Cover Book
Printed in Washington State

What they're saying about Sally's book...

"During the years that I was minister at the Seattle First Baptist Church, followed by my retirement six years ago, I have been privileged to read the newspaper columns that Sally Santana has written. I always found her ideas to be stimulating, insightful and challenging. She has the capability of addressing religious issues and spiritual subjects from a wider universal view, so that the reader can feel both challenged and included in what she writes. This book is a treasure, which will enable one to read and re-read the beautiful spiritual truths that Sally has shared and which she embodies."

Rev. Dr. Rodney Romney
Idaho Falls, ID

"Sally Santana has a way of looking at life that involves creativity, sensitivity, heartfelt sincerity and abundant optimism. Her observations and commentaries on life, love and the foibles of mankind are enjoyable and always give me much to ponder. Sally walks the path of my old friend, the Rev. Dale Turner, the late beloved minister and spiritual essayist. I used to jokingly call her Dale Jr., but she is now carving her own unique path through the wilderness of faith and religion."

Dick Hooper
Retired Corrections Administrator
Shoreline, WA

"Sally Santana is deeply involved in everyday life and writes from her own experience, connecting her struggles with her discoveries of the Holy and making the ignored aspects of our lives come alive for us. She shares reviews of others' writings that have spoken to her, inviting us to partake in the same nourishment with her. And she is the kind of true contemplative who weeps and aches for social justice in the world -- and puts her soul into her life practice as the creator of Forgiveness Day in Washington State. 'The Examined Life - Our Spiritual Journey' sheds a welcome light on our own personal growth."

Nancy R. Smith
Author of "Workplace Spirituality: A Complete Guide for Business Leaders"
Peabody, MA

"Sally brings heart, light, and much understanding of the importance of compassion and forgiveness in her writings. Her candor and honesty reach out and touch me in a way is always delightful and impressive. The issues that face us today demand that we look within and acknowledge our fragilities, our fears—and the strength we can find in connecting to each other and to compassion. Sally's voice encourages each of us to do just that."

Margie Coles
Interfaith Council of Washington
Seattle, WA

"Sally Santana's writings have a gem-like quality to them: her style is simple and elegant; her message radiates clarity and brilliance."

Jamal Rahman, Muslim Sufi minister,
Interfaith Community Church, Seattle, WA
Author of "The Fragrance of Faith - the Enlightened Heart of Islam."

"There has always been an excitement within Sally's messages, her words of wisdom. I say this only because, common sense and the life living Love within Sally's experiences, relayed through her written words, has been expressed so honestly, humorously, fearlessly, and faithfully. They bring to us an opportune companionship and trust in a Living God."

Shirley Meyer
Altos, NM

"Wow! In one volume we have the privilege to pursue, ponder and personalize the mind of one of our own Kitsap County writers. I have known and read Sally Santana's uplifting articles for years. She has stimulated my mind, touched my heart and stretched my ethics to include the whole human race in my prayers and positive actions! Over all this time Sally has been willing to put into black and white many universal truths with creative energy and wonderful insight. I believe that these articles contained herein will change each reader over time into a powerful dynamo filled with the Spirit of "love, joy, peace, patience, kindness, goodness, faithfulness, gentleness and self control . . ." (Galatians 5:22).

Pastor Orv Jacobson
First Lutheran Community Church
Port Orchard, WA

"Sally has a holy and unique gift for making complex questions accessible. She is able, with such joy and gladness, to remind us of God's yearning for peace, reconciliation and justice. She is a doorway for so many people who are seeking a generous, loving and all-embracing God. Sally is a gift!"

The Very Reverend Robert V. Taylor,
Dean, Saint Mark's Episcopal Cathedral
Seattle, WA

"Wonderfully resonant words can be found in the writings of Sally Santana. Resonant with my heart, certainly, and resonant with this moment in time for humankind. For in finding the resonance rather than dissonance we are given an immeasurable gift for our personal and global spiritual evolution. Sally's musings, searchings and wisdom can help us find and build the peace of resonant harmony within us and without."

Margie Hyatt, Minister
West Sound Unity
Bremerton, WA

Acknowledgements

This is only possible, of course, because of my newspaper's willingness to let my voice be heard. So the first "Thank you!" goes to The Kitsap Sun. Let this be a note of encouragement to writers everywhere. All I did was call the paper and ask for a chance to write an occasional religion column. Editor Jim Campbell said send me three to take a look at. Two weeks later my first column ran and they've been running ever since. There are few things more wonderful than being paid to do what you love. Take the risk!

I am very grateful to a great many souls for their contributions to my life. Among the many to thank are my dear friends Shirley Meyer, Jim Bryan, Margie Hyatt, Rod Romney, and Georgena Ingram; my beloved brother Chet; and boundless gratitude and love to my son Gabriel who loves me unconditionally, is a constant inspiration, a terrific conversationalist, and a great man.

Introduction

This column began as a "whenever" thing; it ran as there was room on the religion page, or alternating with another writer. The first couple years you'll see gaps in time between them. This is why.

In the beginning, too, I could write as long an article as I wanted. In 2001, many of us were put on a 500-word diet, so you'll notice the incredibly shrinking column sometime that year. This was very hard to deal with, but I ended up thanking my then editor, JoAnne Marez. Having fewer words to convey what I wanted to forced me to "get to the point" more quickly. And while I couldn't go into as much detail as I did before, it sharpened my writing and packed a better punch. Again... thank you JoAnne.

I wish I'd known I was going to do this from the beginning; it has been a challenge to go back and match up columns with headings and dates. I was missing a floppy disk for a whole year and ended up typing them in. Spending time with these old columns was like visiting with old friends. I would recall where I was when I wrote it, or what was prompting me to write about the subject. In reading them over, I found myself asking myself the questions I did in them. They have renewed my sense of commitment and purpose. May they do so for you, as well.

Please – if you have a comment or insight, or if you'd like to connect over a subject, email me at sally@sallysantana.com

Thank you ~ *Sally*

1999

February 13, 1999

God, like beauty, is in eye of beholder

It's easy to look at a newborn and marvel at the tiny fingers and bellybutton, but how often do you stop to appreciate the delicacy of a dandelion? "A weed? I try to kill them, not care about them", you say.

A story circulated a while back about some Japanese tourists driving from Seattle to Silverdale. They marveled over a government that valued beauty so much it would plant acres of exquisite yellow flowers along the roadway. Scotch broom! Can you imagine? They were in awe of what we consider to be one of the earth's most despicable growths. And yet...the little yellow blooms ARE lovely.

How often do you take the time to marvel at the deep smile wrinkles in your mother's face, or the wagging tail of the beloved family dog? How did all these things come to be? What do they represent?

In his spiritual biography, Fr. Bede Griffiths reflects on how real awareness came upon him. "One day, I walked out alone in the evening and heard the birds singing in full chorus. I remember the shock of surprise with which the sound broke on my ears. It seemed to me that I had never heard the birds singing before, and wondered if they sang like this all year round, and I'd never noticed. Everything then grew still as the sunset faded. A feeling of awe came over me. I felt inclined to kneel on the ground, as though I had been in the presence of an angel; and I hardly dared to look on the face of the sky, because it seemed as though it was but a veil before the face of God."

We are so busy everyday – off to work, kids to baseball, car in the shop, is chicken on sale? You don't have time to be a mystic, you say. You don't have time to watch your child sleep, or a seagull soar? Maybe you equate it with self-indulgent naval gazing?

Allowing yourself to be impressed with the glory of God, however, adds a dimension that delights your soul.

Anyone can be a mystic. It isn't reserved for grand souls from the past. All it means is that you see God everywhere, in everything, in all people. Too hard to swallow? You can't see God in a child molester or a rock? We aren't talking behaviors here. We're looking at the big picture of creation. Our field of vision can be so narrow in so many ways.

Sultan Valad, son of Rumi (the Sufi mystic) says, "A human being must be born twice. Once from his mother, and again from his own existence."

Everyone is created in the image of their Creator, which is to say we all have souls. The invitation to go deeper into the mystery of God is always there. We have free will to pick the path we want to go. To be born from your own experience is to choose to see the world through different eyes.

There is an old saying, "When the student is ready, the teacher appears." The teacher could be an apple, an old car, or a song. You can be a hamster running in a wheel forever, or you can invite the awe and reverence and wonder of God into your existence and allow yourself to be transformed.

"We are here," Vietnamese mystic Thich Nhat Hahn says, "to awaken from the illusion of our separateness."

"I remember this illumination happening to me one noontime," writes Holly Bridges Elliot in "Beholding God in Many Faces", "as I stood in the kitchen and watched my kids eat peanut butter and jelly sandwiches. We were having a most remarkable time on a nondescript day, in the midst of utter routine. I had not sprinkled the place mats with holy water, or uttered a sanctifying prayer over the Wonder Bread. I wasn't feeling particularly spiritual. But, heeding I don't know what prompting, I stopped abruptly in mid-bustle and looked around me as if I were opening my eyes for the first time that day."

She continues, "The entire room became luminous and so alive with movement that everything seemed suspended – yet pulsated – for an instant, like light waves. Intense joy swelled inside me, and my immediate response was gratitude. Gratitude for everything. The shelter of the room became a warm embrace; water flowing from the tap seemed a tremendous miracle; and my children became, for a moment, not my progeny or my charges or tasks, but eternal beings of infinite singularity and complexity whom I would one day, in an age to come, apprehend in their spiritual fullness."

Let go, and let God expand within you.

March 6, 1999

All powerful God still allows us to create plenty of our own disasters

In 1981, Rabbi Harold Kushner wrote a book titled, "When Bad Things Happen To Good People." It was a best seller that asked a question that humanity has been trying to answer for ages.

To some degree, it depends on what your definition of "bad" is. For example, some folks believe capital punishment is wrong under any circumstances. Others disagree. Is there only one answer for God-believing people?

In his book, the Rabbi recounts the day he and his wife learned that their toddler had progeria, or "rapid aging"; that he wouldn't live past his teens. He writes, "It didn't make sense. I had been a good person. More than that, I was living a more deeply religiously committed life than most people I knew. I believed I was following God's ways, doing His work. How could this be happening to my family? If God existed, if he was minimally fair, let alone loving and forgiving, how could this happen to me?

Have you ever felt like he did? Have you ever struggled to find a reason for brutality and tragedy? We're inundated with reports of people perishing in house fires, avalanches, landslides. Every day a meth lab is found. Every day a child dies of malnutrition. Is God in control of the world? Many believe in the saying, "Satan may have won the battle, but God wins the war." Isn't it kind of selfish of them to put us in the middle?

We've all heard or read the comment after someone passes on that God "took" them. Do you really believe God needed your son or niece because he missed him or her in heaven?

The other reason often given is that "the wages of sin is death." There are some really nasty and mean people still walking the earth, and a lot of little human angels that have passed over. We all eventually die.

Believing this gives us a reason for the incomprehensible. It gives us "someone" to blame; someone we hope won't fry us with a bolt of lightning for questioning His authority to do whatever He wants. But it DOES give us an answer for the unknown.

If only we hadn't been taught that "no ills befall the righteous, but the wicked are filled with trouble." (Proverbs 12:21) Because very bad things happen to absolutely wonderful people.

Theologians have struggled with this question ever since we began to hold a concept of a deity that could rule the rain, fertility, etc. The Old Testament most often portrays God as the worst kind possible: vengeful, merciless...the kind of God Rabbi Kushner, and we, grew up with. Even in this day and age, you'd have a hard time finding someone who doesn't wonder why God has abandoned them.

On "Providence," a TV drama, the lead character is turned down for a job at a hospital. As she sits on a park bench, she raises her arms up in frustration and says: "Why are you doing this to me?"

I firmly believe that God can and does guide us if we are receptive. Of course, two people can get totally different directions and be "good" people. How do you resolve this? What does it mean? To your thinking, if someone disagrees with you, are they wrong?

If we weren't to blame God or Lucifer for our troubles, what is left?

We take the earth and make lots of stuff from it: plastic, caustic chemicals, alcohol, etc. For many things, the long-term effects were unknown and we tried to make repairs after the fact. Remember thalidomide? So now we have so much particulate in the air, so many fumes, people driving drunk. We made choices 50 years ago that we are paying for now. We are only now learning how the combinations of chemicals blowing out of smokestacks for years have mutated our genes. Blame God? I don't think so.

I believe that we are co-creators with God. My favorite example of this is that I can't create a seed, but I can plant it. We create alcohol and we die by it. Or petrochemicals. Is it as simple as the choices we make? And how we've altered our bodies by what we put in them? You don't want to see the pain a baby born to a crack addict faces.

For the longest time, whenever I came across the word "fear" in relation to God, such as "The fear of the Lord is the beginning of wisdom," I cross out the "fear" and write in "love." "Love of the Lord is the beginning of wisdom!" Love of God melts your heart, not fear. Think of how you reacted as a kid when your mom said, "just you wait until your father gets home! Maybe you'll think next time and not do that again!" I'm not saying it wasn't a good deterrent, but how much happier life could have been if you didn't glue your sister's pigtails together while she was sleeping because you loved her – and your mom and dad.

It is easier to blame God for the ills of the world, sometimes, than face up to the choices we have made.

March 20, 1999

Relationships are important

Do you have a personal relationship with Jesus the Christ? And what exactly does that mean? What are the criteria? How do you know if you have one? Is it "to know, love, and serve God in this world and the next?" Is it acknowledging Jesus as your Lord and savior? How do you define it? And do you need it?

I have heard preachers say that you're supposed to have one, but I haven't heard them say how you'd know it when you got it.

If you go beneath the surface, the question arises: how can you have a "personal" relationship with a deity on another plane of existence? And if Jesus is there, and you can communicate with him, why not others?

Maybe we should start out by defining "personal." I think we cold agree that it has to do with you. It's not a generic thing. It's something YOU have. I don't mean to belabor the point, but do let it sink in.

"Relationship." You have them, even in your sleep! The depth, however, is a determining factor.

You have a relationship with the checker at the grocery store. You may even know his name. Perhaps you have a child care provider. Chances are you've done some checking on their qualifications, so you know them a little better. How about your kids? You spend time with them, and you love and care for them, but its not like you can share your fears with your five year old.

What about your spouse, parents, or best friend? These are probably the most intimate, equal relationships you have. You would most likely use one of these to help you discover whether or not you have a truly personal relationship with Jesus.

Look at your relationship with your best friend. You tell each other your history over time, listening and living with them through the tough and wonderful times. And its give and take. You discuss the most important to the most mundane matters. You give each other the benefit of your opinion and wisdom. You can't imagine life without them, they are so much a part of your thinking, your behavior, your planning. You take pleasure in their company, and they do yours. In essence, you open yourself up totally, heart and soul, to a person you know will honor your trust and commitment. They seem like an extension of you; they are a part of you, and you love them dearly.

In light of this, can you determine what kind of relationship you have with Jesus? Is He an acquaintance to you, or your best friend? Is He at a distance, or a daily part of your life. In your heart of hearts, do you think it's impossible to have any kind of relationship with Him because of who He is and where He is?

Everybody's experience will be different. If you want to have a personal relationship with Jesus, all I recommend is that you take a leap of faith and ask Him to make Himself known to you in an undeniable way. And then listen and watch.

April 10, 1999

Our 'father' in heaven? Well, maybe

Faith is mysterious. Chip Brown, in his book, "Afterwards, You're A Genius", says, "Beliefs can be shaken, but faith is the result of being shaken..."

Have you ever seen God?

Not in a glance at a baby or a view of the ocean, but toe-to-toe with God? People and stories and books have told you about God but have the two of you sat together with lattés to discuss your latest heartbreak? No? So how do you know God exists?

You can't see air, yet you couldn't live without it. You can't see love or hate, but you do see what we believe to be the manifestation of them.

Jesus is reported to have said, "To see me is to see the Father." We have, then, "seen" God, manifest as Jesus the Christ. But the Father remains invisible, unseen.

The picture of God passed down through the centuries is one of an old European make with long white hair and beard, and intimidating eyes. Is this God? "Of course not," you say. But you can't say what God IS.

In the Upper Room, Jesus appears to the disciples, but Thomas isn't sure this is him, come back from the dead.

Jesus, we're told, didn't come through a door – he just materialized out of thin air. But this wasn't enough for Thomas.

Jesus says, "Put your fingers in my side where the blade pierced me, and believe."

He then says to the group, "You have seen and believed. Blessed are those who haven't seen, yet believe."

I've read that Jesus came in male form and presented the Creator as male because females were to be seen and not heard. They were liabilities on tax returns.

What chance would a woman have at that time, in that culture, to be taken seriously?

Do you believe that God is a man? Our songs and prayers all refer to "Him," and a good reason is because it's almost impossible to take an "it" seriously.

It's hard to fear or love an "it." But a father – that we can relate to. It's hard to wrap your heart around a faceless thing. We're constantly assigning human qualities to everything from cars to coffee because it engages our emotions, our relatedness.

Recently, I attended a Bible study with a friend. The pastor said that women were the reason Jesus had to die; if Eve hadn't coerced Adam into disobeying and taking a bite of the fruit, sin wouldn't have entered the world and Jesus the Christ, God Incarnate, wouldn't have had to suffer. Women were the cause of sin in the world.

We have done untold damage to many women by leaving them out of the picture of God. Are women inherently less in God's eyes because God made them that way?

I was told of a situation at a local church. Third-graders were discussing what they wanted to be when they grew up. One girl said she wanted to be a pastor. A boy said she couldn't be. "Why not?" she asked. "Because only boys can be pastors because God is a man." Crushed, she went to her teacher.

"That's not true, is it?" Not wanting to hurt her, yet needing to tell the truth, the teacher said, "Yes, it is."

This is 1999.

I was miserable for years, believing that I was not loved equally by God.

Did God bother to count all the hairs on my head? Was my name written in the Book of Life? Did I matter? Didn't Jesus come for me, too?

We talk about little girls growing up with low self-esteem. It starts right here. What do we teach our kids about God?

The bottom line is that no one we know of has seen God the Father in the flesh, perhaps because God is neither male nor female and it's in our souls that we image God.

All we have is what has been passed down to us.

"Blessed are those who have not seen, yet believe."

April 17, 1999

Let Jesus lead way at any age

Times are touch for teens. Reflecting back to my high school days in the early 70's, and comparing that to my son's graduation last year, it's clear that life and expectations have changed dramatically.

When the dogs came through to sniff lockers at East High School, it was an alarming event for many of us. These days, while not common, it's no surprise.

The technology explosion has created demands upon our kids that we, as adults, may not always be quick to pick up on.

The bar has been raised for those seeking certain scholarships, for example. You are expected to hold down a part-time job, volunteer in your community, participate in any number of school clubs or activities and maintain a 3.7 grade-point average.

Are we raising teens that are going to crash and burn at 40 because they're burnt out from going 120 mph through life instead of 60? What can we do to alleviate the stresses our kids face? What can they do to help themselves?

You may have seen them on necks, fingers, and wrists: items with WWJD or FROG written on them. They help youth focus, I'm told, on what really matters – the highest priorities.

WWJD is "What Would Jesus Do?" Continued exposure to a lesson embeds itself so that eventually it occurs without conscious thought. Therefore, wearing something that constantly reminds you of God is a good thing.

Teens I've talked to say it helps them to stay chaste (not in those words) or not do drugs: "Jesus didn't huff so I, like, avoid it."

One said it helped him to be honest with himself and others.

FROG is "Fully Rely On God." Put the two together and they can be of real help to today's overwhelmed kids, gentle reminders that there is someone available to connect with you can help you maintain your health and balance.

It's hard to know what Jesus would do if you haven't studied his life. And even then, not everything about him made it onto a page or into the Bible. It can be difficult to translate events from 2,000 years ago to today.

For example, we read that Jesus separated himself from a caravan and took off at age 12, causing his parents and others great fear and distress. When found on the steps of the temple, he remarked, "Surely you know I must be about my Father's business."

From here we say, "Whatever happened to the commandment to "Honor your father and mother?" There are so many things our kids are exposed to that Jesus didn't have to deal with. When kids ask me about this, I tell them you have a scripture and the Holy Spirit to help you. The scripture is Matthew 22:37-40.

"This is the greatest and first commandment: love God with your whole heart, your whole soul, and your whole mind. And the second is similar: you must love your neighbor as yourself. On these two commandments hang the whole law and the prophets, also."

And the Holy Spirit helps you from age to age to understand what it means for you. Discernment is necessary; we can fool ourselves if we ask but don't seek with an open heart and soul. And then trust that God, for whom "nothing is impossible," will help you find what is the highest and best for you.

Hugh Prather, in his book, "Spiritual Notes to Myself: Essential Wisdom for the 21st Century" says, "God speaks to us in a thousand voices, each one with the same clear message: 'I love you. Please trust me on this one.'"

"Fully Rely On God" helps implement WWJD. Being fully reliant doesn't mean you'll get everything you pray for, or that "bad" things won't happen to you. But it can mean that God is your solace when you're hurting; that God, who created humanity and is witness to the joy and pain we cause each other, understands like no other.

My life, like yours, has had its tragedies. Shortly after my mother passing away, I was lying on the living room floor, sobbing into a pillow, and yelling at God, "What good are you? You aren't here to hold me like a human being. You aren't here to help me think clearly or soften my agony!"

The doorbell rang, and after wiping off my face, I opened the door. It was a friend I hadn't seen in years. She opened her arms to me and said, "I read your mother's obituary..."

Here was my God, in the flesh, real and present, loving and sustaining me, which helped me do the same for my son.

Asking yourself what Jesus would do in any situation isn't just for youth.

Perhaps you're bidding on a project and come in low, even though you know you'll be over budget later. Do you tell just a little white lie to avoid embarrassment or humiliation?

What would Jesus do?

June 12, 1999

Worry won't change things, so give God a chance instead

You probably have a "life lesson" or two that you share with your family or hold close in your memory because it reminds you of its outcome.

I used to be a worrier (far more than I am now.) I was taught to analyze and prepare for all negative possibilities; that way you wouldn't be taken by surprise and would stand a better chance of survival. It was difficult to enjoy life.

In the late 80's, I picked up a book at the library on Buddhism. It talked about "being present" and "detachment." I remember asking God to help me understand this. Then I had the following experience:

A dear friend of mine was told late on a Friday afternoon that he was to report to the superior first thing Monday morning.

"Reduction in force," we both thought aloud. His time had come to get his pink slip. He was worried – he had a new bride and a new house. Lots of card payments. What would they do?

On Monday morning, before he went in to see the boss, we prayed together at his desk. He said that he and the missus had crunched numbers all weekend and were worn out; they had prayed for guidance but hadn't "heard" anything yet.

With a heavy heart, he went to his meeting. Twenty minutes later he was at my desk, grinning from ear to ear. No pink slip for my friend – he was being reclassified so they could keep him where he was, with expanded duties.

This event was pivotal for me in my life. It pointed out in stark relief how I was living. I paused to ponder – maybe 10% of everything I "prepared" for by worrying actually happened.

I had spent a good chunk of my life getting ready for the "inevitable" that never happened. I discovered it did no good to worry about a probability.

What worrying did, however, was flood my body with tension-producing chemicals like cortisol (fight or flight). I always was on edge, always looking at things from 10 different angles. And it did me no good at all.

Matthew 6:25 came home to me.

"That is why I am telling you not to worry about your life and what you are to eat, or about your body and how you are to clothe it.

Look at the birds in the sky. They don't sow or gather into barns. Yet your Father feeds them. Can any of you, for all your worrying, add a minute to your life?

Set your hearts on the kingdom and on his righteousness, and all these things will be given you as well. So don't fret about tomorrow; it will take care of itself. Each day has enough trouble of its own."

No kidding!

For me, this was "being present." Fully participating in the day I was living. It's not like you can't plan ahead, but when you listen, you fully listen – you're not just waiting for someone to finish speaking so you can.

If you're not busy fretting, you bring all your skills and creativity to bear on whatever situation you're facing.

"Detachment" at this point had more to do with what I chose to get all worked up over. Not all concerns are life or death. None of them ever had been. At that time, it had to do with prioritizing what would get my attention. I had to be more discerning and selective of what I did dwell on.

About this time, I was introduced to the writing of Joel Goldsmith. I don't agree with everything he wrote in his lifetime, but his book "Infinite Supply" turned me around and had me looking at God with more faith and hope.

I have since read everything he has written. Not coming from a financially secure background and doing without a lot of basics most of my growing up years, I found it hard to see God in the messes we found ourselves in. But confronting these old experiences and beliefs was a turning point for me.

What did I really believe about God? What kind of God did I believe in? One that I had to be fearful of, or one that loved me and wanted to help if asked?

I believe God can lead each of us if we only be quiet long enough for god to get a word in. We think we know best, and that is not always the case.

"Let go and let God," is not a useless phrase. So don't worry, be happy!"

June 19, 1999

What you think can have immediate effect

"You create your own reality" could be the theme of the New Age movement, which a lot of people avoid like the plague.

But like a lot of things in life, there is a kernel of truth to it.

Oftentimes, we dismiss something because we disapprove of the source – "Can anything good come from Nazareth?" – and miss out on something worthwhile because we have a prejudice.

Saying that you, to a certain degree, "create your own reality" does not in any way negate God, Jesus, or the Bible. Indeed, we were created with free will.

Every single person who ever lived created, in part, their reality, their circumstances.

We do this with every decision we make and execute, by our thoughts and by what we choose to put into our minds, bodies, and environment. By being pessimistic or optimistic.

So to dismiss this statement out of hand as having no validity because you associate it with something you fear or dislike is to miss an opportunity for growth.

I have read of those who believe that everything you experience you create, but I disagree with that. We have been polluting our air with all manner of carcinogens for years, and now we reap what we have collectively sown in the form of respiratory ailments and cancers. Humanity as a whole has created these situations.

A country decides to go to war and drafts a young man right out of high school. He is taught how to kill the enemy and is shipped overseas.

In order to stay alive he must take another's life which goes against everything he has ever been taught. "Conscientious objector" were not words in his vocabulary.

People would have thought him less than patriotic if he had fled to Canada, anyway. He had to make some serious choices. But he did have them.

Mind-body medicine, as explained by Dr. Candace Pert ("Molecules of Emotion") and Caroline Myss ("Why People Don't Heal") deal specifically with the effects of thoughts on our physical bodies.

The observation that "thoughts are things" is valid because what you think can have an instantaneous effect, and if you dwell on something repeatedly you can cause your body to experience an imbalance of chemicals, hormones, etc. and contribute to the creation of illness.

So how will you create your reality today and tomorrow?

Will you cruise pornographic Web sites at work and be fired? Will you be a victim in a car accident and carry hatred for the other driver all your life? Will you set time aside every day to pray for guidance?

Guard your thoughts; they are not created equal. If the notion to gossip – no matter how benign the content may be – enters your mind, consider how you would feel if you were overhearing such a conversation about you.

Instead of giving in to despair about your finances, be proactive and honest with yourself. What did I do to get into this mess (went berserk with credit cards, now "they" call day and night)? What can I do to get out of it (cut up cards, contact counseling)? And how can I keep from coming back to this point (delay gratification, save, live with a budget)?

You make decisions and people associated with you make decisions that create your reality.

To a good degree, you are the captain of your ship. Will you allow your thoughts and behavior to ride you into the rocks, or will you consciously steer your boat, mindful of the tides and icebergs?

Being able to think, to process information and act on decisions, is a gift from God. If we are to be good stewards of the earth and ourselves, we need to pay attention to what we create, either through design or default.

We choose to forgive or let anxiety rule. We choose to teach peace, or promote violence. It's up to us.

I believe we are co-creators with our Creator. Our collective thoughts and behaviors have created the world we live in, and we can change it the same way.

Let's start by lifting our thoughts to God at noon, every day, for one minute. Just one minute at the same time every day.

Our focused prayer, like a laser beam, will be that God's will be done. Period.

God knows what we need, and will provide us with the guidance and power to make whatever course corrections are required to make his will manifest.

We have been given a mind-boggling opportunity by God to change our world. Who will you serve this day?

June 26, 1999

What's in a name? Ask Falwell

The Rev. Jerry Falwell's organization has come out against Lilith Fair, a traveling concert of women performers.

The story goes in ancient Jewish literature that Lilith was the first wife of Adam. She rebelled against his authority and asserted her independence.

Why did God allow this in the sacred garden? Why does God keep sending Adam "uppity" women? Eve was pretty strong-willed, too.

Versions of the story differ; but one says that she then left Adam and became a demon. This, I take it, is the reason some Christians are upset.

Are they afraid that this musical event will inspire women to mutiny? Give them impetus to rebel? Or perhaps it had to do with putting thoughts of "demons" out into the world.

But that can't be it because we use the words "Satan," "devil" or "Lucifer" at most services in a church or on TV.

This story doesn't seem so far-fetched, even for today: Assert yourself, woman, and see what can happen!

What does Falwell's organization hope to do by raising the alarm about these concerts? What does it hope it accomplish? Is it to warn people away from good music?

I doubt that the creator of Lilith Fair, Sarah McLachlan, picked the name because she knew it would lead people from a segment of the Christian population astray.

Her publicist says the name was chosen because Lilith represented independence and freedom to McLachlan, and the tour of women musicians was unique.

I don't mean to pick on the Rev. Falwell. His is just one of the many voices that continue to assert that women should remain submissive to their husbands – or any male, really.

Don't we tell the small son (not daughter) of any woman, "You take care of mommy, now," as if a 3 year-old boy had more sense and wisdom than a woman?

What a burden this is to the little tyke who takes these words literally. Isn't the adult supposed to take care of the child?

And to those who state they can't change this teaching because it's in the Bible, I tell them to check out 1 Corinthians 6"1-8. There are lots of "good Christians" who take each other to court. There are lots of verses that we ignore because they don't serve God, in our estimation, anymore.

I've been told that someone in the house has to have the last word, and it has to be the man because he was made first, and woman came from man.

On "Sesame Street," we all learned to "compromise" and "prioritize." Have we forgotten so soon?

All sorts of interesting questions come to mind.

Since Adam was created from the mind of God, does that make him God incarnate? And he sinned (according to the Bible). Now what?

We pick and choose which laws to follow all the time. We don't go by Leviticus anymore.

"We've got refrigeration now, weirdo. Things have changed."

Exactly!

Please don't send any hate mail my way. I'm just asking questions.

How much do you know about Jewish history? The people, customs, practices? Their politics and religion?

Any time you "receive" guidance from God, it comes to you through your filters – your religious training, experience, beliefs.

God did not put pen to papyrus and write the Bible down. God inspired many people to record their stories that ended up selected by men and placed in this book.

Do I hate men? No. I just take the panoramic view from today backward and see whom "truths" like this serve.

If done with what I believe was the original intent (spouses care for each other with love and respect, not one "lording" all the rights and responsibilities over the other), that is one thing.

But that is not how things have generally worked out. My ex used to tell me when I could go to the store, which one, whether or not I could go to church, etc. This is an abuse of power.

If we choose to align our hearts and minds to God as fully and honestly as we can, we can be living conduits of our creator. The trouble is, lots of people believe they have received a word of knowledge or direction from God.

This includes folks like Jim Jones, Heaven's gate members and others.

I have some wonderful friends, a couple, who struggle with this issue. She says, "How could God do this to us? Does it mean that he created us with some inborn inability to discern wisdom?"

Paul writes to Timothy, "I do not give a woman permission to teach a man anything or tell him what to do. A woman ought not to speak because Adam was first and Eve afterwards, and it was not Adam who was led astray, but the woman.

"Nevertheless, she will be saved by childbearing, provided she lives a modest life and is constant in her faith and love and holiness."

There it is, in the New Testament. Do you believe this as truth? That would mean, then, that all women unable to conceive and carry a child to term will not be "saved."

Is this one of those directions you would choose to ignore or rationalize away? The whole Lilith issue takes on a new light when placed in the context of today.

I saw a bumper sticker recently that said "Uppity Women Unite!" I think God for uppity, assertive women like Hildegard of Bingen, Joan of Arc, Mother Teresa and Elizabeth Dole.

October 9, 1999

Placing ethics, morals

Don't you just wish sometimes that God would break through the hustle and bustle of your life and yell directions at you? Because if a direction came from The Big Guy himself, with no ambiguity, you'd know you couldn't go wrong.

No matter what way something turned out, you'd be in God's will, which is what a lot of people want to be. Sort of like a heavenly insurance policy.

But that doesn't happen often.

We aren't perfect vessels. We're human beings with a teeny spark of divinity in us which we're (hopefully) fanning all the time.

And how do you fan your tiny speck of "spark"?

One answer would be that your behavior be ethically and morally sound. Our society has a lot of absolutes, but also a lot of gray area. For example, one culture believes that anyone caught stealing must forfeit a hand. We do things differently.

You may strive to "do to others as you'd like done to you" in your personal life. Basic golden rule stuff. But does this translate to your business dealings?

If you're in business, you're there to make a profit. At what cost, though, to yourself, to those that sell your products and produce them?

Doesn't it then become more a "dog eat dog" thing? In order to increase your profit margin, must you sacrifice your integrity?

Lately I've been reading responsible articles on mega-retailers that provide us with low, low prices. They (retailer) can do it because the item was constructed by a kid in a Third World country working for a few cents an hour.

If you knew the warm sweatshirt you bought at that ridiculously low price was sewn together by an 8-year-old girl in a Mexican sweatshop, would it make a difference? Or would you justify it to yourself with, "That's normal for their culture," or "It's none of my business."

What about the child's life? Would you want that for your own kids? We all know how boycotts can change how business is done. Would you be willing to pay a little more if it was made in America?

We spend a lot of time in this country talking about family values. About what is morally and ethically sound.

Are these goals only for the other guy? Where is God in all this? Where is God in management? Is God separated from how we do business?

How would you feel if you were on the other end of your decisions? The heart of the situation is, do you "love God with your whole heart, your whole soul, your whole mind and all your strength?"

Because if you do it will come through in every facet of your life; it would be evident in everything you do.

December 11, 1999

Forgiveness: gift that returns

This Christmas, consider giving yourself a gift.

Most often, when we give this particular gift, we think it benefits others more than it does us. It isn't a family trip to Hawaii in February or volunteering for a worthwhile committee. It's forgiveness.

No one you need to forgive? Let's see...Do you still do a slow burn when you think of the teacher who gave your kid a D in math when she had worked so hard to break a C? What about the doctor who talked about your mother as if she weren't there when you came by to visit her in the nursing home? Or the anonymous person who "keyed" your car? They don't have to be major transgressions.

Forgiveness can either cost you nothing and be given with joy, or it can feel as though you're having a root canal – with no anesthesia.

Some folks feel that, if they forgive someone for hurting them or a loved one, they somehow condone the behavior. Not true. Or that they betray the victim by not hanging on to anger and hate. Who does that benefit? Do you think all the chemicals your emotions are flooding your bloodstream with affect anybody but you? Is the offender spending sleepless nights worried about what you think about him? Is the offender increasing the tight frown lines in his face because you're in such distress? I don't think so. All your unforgiveness does is hurt you and set a poor example of God's love.

We can all talk a good story when pushed to the wall. We refer to Jesus' words on the cross, "Father forgive them for they know not what they do," as if we weren't called upon to do the same thing.

Maybe it was your son or brother or mother who was murdered. Or your sister's husband who was laid off, causing them to lose their home. Perhaps it was your Christmas lawn decorations that were stolen. Do you think you're making the perpetrator pay by not letting go of the anger you carry in your gut and soul? Is holding on to resentment and desperation going to bring your loved one back to life? Absolutely not.

So, what good is forgiveness?

You must forgive for your own health. Forgetting is optional. For some, to forget means to keep going back into abusive relationships that a person is better off staying out of or ignoring the facts of history and doing the same thing over again. Sometimes, it's not good to forget and run the risk of losing the lesson that came from an event.

I made an acquaintance very mad at me a couple of years ago – so mad that this person didn't speak to me for an entire year. To my way of thinking, I had done absolutely nothing wrong. But to this person, I had violated something they held dear. One day, this person spoke to me. It wasn't anything earth shattering; they were testing the waters. I responded and smiled. I don't know who felt better. To this day, I am profoundly grateful that I was forgiven. It doesn't matter who was right. We are now "right" with each other.

I'm not saying that you should pretend that life is all peachy-keen and rosy when it's not. It takes time to grieve, and you should go through it and not around it because unexpended grief can torture you just like failing to forgive can.

There comes a time, however, when the light of God's love can reach a frozen heart and give the opportunity to let it rest. You owe it to yourself, your family, your co-workers and the supermarket checker to release your anxiety to God and let God work on healing all those involved.

The cover of a recent "Spirituality and Health" magazine had on it a picture of three middle-aged men, arm in arm, in front of the Vietnam War Memorial, heads bent together.

One of the men says to another "Have you forgiven your captors yet?"

The man in the middle says "No! I'll never forgive them for what they did to me!"

The third man then says "It looks like they still hold you captive, then."

You may never forget, but you can forgive.

In honor of Jesus' birthday this year, do something special. Do something he would appreciate. Set the captive free – you.

2000

January 22, 2000

Living in luxury:
What would Jesus think of today's Christians?

My mother raised me to believe that a good Christian is a poor one. She pointed to the life of Jesus, St. Francis of Assisi's renunciation of wealth, and Mother Teresa, among others. They had what they needed but little else. By choice. Boy, have things changed!

I have struggled most of my adult life with wanting a better (read: materialistic) existence, yet not wanting to have too much. But who is to say how much is too much? Compared to the names listed above, I live in luxury, even though I live in low-income housing.

Jesus' friends supplied his needs as his ministry progressed. Today, we'd call him a freeloader or worse, living off the largess of others. And those who helped him probably would be called enablers – he'd made his choices, let him face the music those choices created.

We can assume he expected his Abba to provide for his needs, and aid came through those who loved him, allowing him to carry out his "Father's business" without having to do the 9 to 5 thing in the carpentry shop.

A couple of weeks ago, I saw a televangelist teaching that God wanted all his children to have "every good thing," and he backed it up with a lot of scripture. He said there was nothing wrong with limo service and a roast on the table every night. Private schools for the kids. Air Jordans. Nothing but the best! And if God should provide enough money for the minister to wear Armani, so be it!

We could say that we haven't been called to the same course of ministry as Jesus (savior – a one of a kind job), so we don't need to live the kind of austere life he did. We've been called to different types of ministry: parent, teacher, musician, paid ministry. In all of those, and in all other avenues in which we bring our "Christianity" to bear, aren't we called to be our brother's keeper? To love others as we would want to be loved? To love "our neighbor as ourself?"

How much is too much? At what point do we recognize greed? And would being greedy bother us?

This TV minister went on to say that a Jesus who had poor followers wouldn't attract many others. But if you worship Jesus AND you own a Lexus, well... THAT'S the kind of God to follow. I kid you not.

I'm sure we'd all defend our current lifestyle, not wanting to give up any of the goodies we have and worked so hard for. But let's not forget the story of Jesus being tempted with the riches of the world. "All this will be yours if you follow me."

Have we sold our souls for a newer car? An Armani suit? A face lift? I'm not saying that we aren't to enjoy the gifts that have been created for our use and enjoyment.

Jesus partied, too, and enjoyed some of the finer things in life. But I am wondering about the balance we have in our lives today.

Are we in the world, but not of it?

If you've recognized that your lifestyle goes for instant gratification and self-indulgence, and you want to make a change, consider these ideas:

If you normally buy three or four bags of chips, a couple six packs of beer, a bottle of wine, three magazines and four cartons of cigarettes a month, estimate the cost and write a check to your local food bank for at least half that amount. Budget it in.

Perhaps you pay $25 a month to your gym, and the same amount for your Internet service. Send the same amount every other month to the "Y" of your choice so they can give a scholarship to a needy kid for a healthy activity.

Use your imagination.

If you're going to Hawaii for a week...

Well, just ask yourself, "What would Jesus do?"

March 18, 2000

'God's will be done' but who knows how?

You might not have thought of it this way before, but we are in the process of creating our own evolution.

The theory of evolution contends that we, in an effort to adapt to ever changing environmental and perhaps sociological needs, have altered our DNA over the ages in order to survive.

Some "thing" triggered this response in us in the past, but we're now not waiting to see what will happen over time.

We know this desire to live extends from viruses to every creature swimming or running for its life, including us two-legged types trying to avoid the effects of earthquakes, age, and disease. Everything wants to live, to save itself, and it will develop the means to do so.

Look at the panic we're in these days. A lot of our antibiotics don't work anymore. The "bugs" they killed off have mutated in such a way that the "key" in the antibiotic doesn't fit the "lock" on the bacteria, and so they live on.

Did God create all forms of life with a shelf life? Have all our efforts to maintain good health and extend our lives interfered with the "Master Plan?" What are we tinkering with?

Don't get me wrong. As a Type 2 diabetic, I am grateful to be alive every day, and thankful for the science that permits that.

Hippocrates wrote, "Make a habit of two things – to help, or at least do no harm." We have no way of knowing whether we are or not, in the short run. Every time we introduce a genetically altered vegetable, animal, or person, we change so many equations in ways we may not recognize for hundreds of years.

Scientists can place enzymes inside DNA that can alter their outcome. Those that have struggled to create frost resistant fruit, grow sheets of skin, or cure cystic fibrosis believe in its value.

In the March issue of Discover, scientist Francis Collins, one of the Human Genome Project's chief researchers (the project that is mapping the sequencing of our 46 chromosomes) says that, "Everything we do-from the time we're a one-celled embryo until adulthood – and all the ways we fight off disease or fall victim to them will be illuminated by understanding these instructions (DNA)."

You may ask, "How can knowing how to create something from the test tube up be bad if it's going to save lives?" Depends on who is doing it. The ways and means of accomplishing these goals aren't restricted to those who share your moral or ethical values. It can be used for very bad as well as very good purposes. What constraints are we putting in place? Is there truly anything we can do to prevent some "mad scientist" from creating a superhuman to compete on the battlefield or ball field?

KCTS ran a program in January, hosted by Alan Alda, titled "Scientific American Frontiers." Together we marveled as we entered labs that were developing the technology to duplicate, for example, a single heart cell into a whole, implantable heart.

The news regularly reports of people willing to pay astronomical prices for the egg of a woman who fits their criteria of "perfection."

What are we doing?

Now, God gave us the brains to figure out how to do this. Does that make it the right thing to do? How are we to know whether what we're doing (there is quite a controversy brewing on fetal tissue research, for example) is in the ultimate best interest of humanity? That it's "God's will"? Are we doing what is ethically and morally sound? Is there no limit to our ingenuity? How far is too far?

We will all be the recipients of this technology as time goes on. Whether it's the type of insulin you use, skin grafts you need, food you ingest or the heart beating in your chest, you will be a part of the evolution.

When asked, "Has your work as a geneticist ever conflicted with your faith?" Collins replied, "No. For me, being involved in the genome project seems illuminated by faith. As someone who believes in a personal God, I find that the opportunity to uncover some of the mysteries of human biology is also an opportunity for worship.

What do you think?

March 25, 2000

What do home and soul mean to you?

Recently, I was in the women's room at Barnes and Noble. There was a mom, her baby and a grandma in the stall next to me. The newborn was wailing as only a newborn can. In my mind's eye, I could see the tiny chin quivering uncontrollably. One of my son's first nicknames was "Jitter Chin." In time, I know he will forgive me for telling you this.

The infant's diaper was being changed, and the two mothers cooed and chatted while the decibel level held steady.

Somehow, in my mind, the bellow was translated into plain English and this is what I "heard.":

"Who in their right mind would want to begin life like this? There's no dignity! I'm unable to care for myself, totally dependent on others for my very survival. This situation is totally unsatisfactory!"

Suddenly the child was silent. Snaps were connected, the diaper bag closed. But the little one's frustration had not been fully discharged. There was a deep intake of breath and then a loud, angry squall.

The women were puzzled; baby was clean and dry and otherwise OK. But I heard something else entirely: "I wanna go back home!"

Home. It could be where you were born or where you live now, or where you feel safe and accepted – a favorite hangout. When I was a youngster moving about the country, home to me was the nearest library.

Take a moment and consider where your soul comes from. Heaven? Do you ever cogitate on your beginnings?

The true essence of you, when your earthly adventure ends, will return from whence it came. Your tour of duty up, your soul will (as far as anyone can know) return to its home port.

When you do end up back at the beginning and find yourself at the cinema with a big box of buttered popcorn and your favorite soda watching the movie highlights of your life, how will you feel? Would you give it a thumbs up or down?

"But, wait!", you cry. "I don't know what the criteria for a 'good life' is!"

Personally, I think that knowledge is hard-wired into us (soul) and we make choices through our lives that support or suppress it.

I know when the lights go down and the reel on my life whirs, I will be seeing flashbacks frames in these terms: "Did you love Me as best you could? Did you recognize Me in others? Did you revere all forms of life and marvel at my geraniums and giraffes? Did you appreciate all the good others did for you, and tell them how wonderful they were? Did you accept responsibility for your thoughts and actions?" This should be interesting!

Are there things you'd like to change? You never know how much time is left.

We should all slow down enough to consider what's true and real and always try to understand the way other people feel.

We should be less quick to anger and show appreciation more. And love the people in our lives like we've never loved before.

April 1, 2000

Spread a little love in the spirit of Jesus

So you think you'd know Jesus when he returns? You'd welcome him with open arms, on bended knee?

Jesus didn't come to create a new religion but to reveal God. To pull people away from paths that led to dead spiritual ends.

On the one hand, we say we are to emulate Jesus' life and lifestyle. On the other, we're totally into greed. We teach our kids in Sunday school and confirmation classes that it is better to give than receive, yet we're not conspicuous as adults at passing up instant gratification.

So you think you'd be thrilled and overjoyed at Jesus' return? I don't think so. If there are ANY needy seniors in your church community, shame on you. If there are ANY children hungry or in need of a coat or school supplies, shame on you. If you aren't in a position to meet a need by yourself, you can bring others together and find out how to help. Even if you can't afford a bag of groceries, you can afford a bag of rice. If you can't afford a coat, you can get four other folks who can pitch in. There is almost nothing worse than being anonymous and unloved in church. So how are you doing?

Are you still eager for Jesus to return? Would you recognize him if he came as a her? If he came out of Iran? Isn't it true that if anyone were to walk the Earth and say they were Jesus, we'd find a way to lock them up?

What's that? You say Jesus will come with signs and wonders? Others can, too, or so I've heard. So how are we going to recognize God when God chooses to be seen in a body on this planet again?

Look in the mirror.

I'm thinking maybe we'll hear something like, "Did you feed me when you saw I was hungry? Did you turn your back on me when you found out I was gay? Did you clean out the gutters and repair my roof after I broke my hip? Did you even know I needed help? Did you know I existed?

How did Jesus live day to day? Who took care of him while he was on the road working for his dad? What impact did he have on his times and why? Where did he sleep? How, where, when and why did he pray?

Jesus made a lot of people mad because he challenged the status quo. What makes us think we'd do any better now? Even Jesus knew that what he was to do and be would involve self-denial and sacrifice, but also give him great joy and happiness. Even the poorest among us has something to give, to share.

What's to prevent you from taking a fatherless child to a Mariner game with your family? Or helping a senior cover the cost of a prescription (church secretaries know everything – they'll know who could use a helping hand.) Open your eyes and take a good, close look at the people around you. What do you see in the widower's or single mom's eyes? Could they use a smile? Introduce yourself and ask them to sit with you after service, have a cup of coffee and share. Draw them out.

What's keeping you from saying no to one more committee meeting and helping your kids with their homework instead, or having an extended dinner at home with your spouse? Like the old saying goes, "Generosity begins at home."

You don't even have to give 'til it hurts – just give. Give your money, your time, your prayers, your non judgmental spirit and willing soul. Give the gift of really listening, not merely waiting for someone to take a breath so you an put your 12 cents in. Listen with your heart. It's a precious, generous thing to do, and rarely happens. In the gospel of Matthew, Jesus is asked what the greatest law is. "To love God with your whole heart, your whole soul, and your whole mind. The second is like it – love your neighbor as yourself. On these two hang the laws of all the prophets."

What does it mean to love God? Read it again, slowly. Get inside it. Breathe it. Feel it. Let your soul bask in its maker's love. It will blow your mind.

God is love.

May 20, 2000

Your being here now is important

Do you recall Peggy Lee's hit, "Is That All There Is?" In it, she lays out a series of life circumstances with the refrain, "If that's all there is my friend, then let's keep dancing/Let's break out the booze and have a ball/If that's all...there is."

Is this all there is to life? Wake up. School, work, or both. Maybe marriage and kids. Sleep. Taxes. Death. Day after day of routine.

Why are you here on this planet sucking in oxygen, exhaling carbon dioxide? What purpose does your living serve?

Perhaps you're fortunate enough to have some inkling of your life's purpose. There are lots of books that can help you discover or define what it is. But I'm talking about the bigger picture.

We've all heard about those spy satellites that can clearly see a slug on your garden from five miles up. Imagine you're the camera on that satellite. Pull back a notch. There's the 7/11 and your cul-de-sac. Back another notch. That must be I-5 and maybe the Sea-Tac airport. You've lost sight of anything smaller than huge now. Go back a couple settings. Wow! You're near the moon! There's North America. You can see how light is being held in around the Earth. Your sense of reality is shifting. Thoughts of orthodontia and electric bills leave your mind.

Back it up again. The Earth is a blue and white marble seemingly supported by nothing. It crosses your mind that you are one of many billions on that planet. That life isn't limited to humans; it includes trees, viruses, societies and thoughts. "Pure energy," Spock said on Star Trek. How does the Earth just "be" like that? Why doesn't it fall? But then – what way would be down? You've lost your bearings, but gained something you can't fully define yet.

As you gaze at the entire Earth, just beginning to get some handle on your overwhelming emotions, you turn away. At 180 degrees your view extends into the blackness. Coming through to you from hundreds of light years away is the light from something you saw on a Web site: (http://antwrp.gsfc.nasa.gov/apod/as950626.html). It's the M100, a spiral galaxy. "Oh, my God!" you whisper to no one.

There is no time, no night or day. No up or down. This is as real as being stuck in traffic in Gorst.

We came from stardust and to stardust we shall return.

Your being here at this point in time is very important. It doesn't look like God neglected any details. Believe that you are a one-of-a-kind original, with specific and unique qualities. What you are and have to give is like no other. You may think that, because of your age, past or infirmity, or your lack of self-esteem, that you can't make a meaningful contribution. Maybe someone has told you that your ideas are worthless or not as good as theirs. That simply isn't true. Because they aren't you.

A lot of life is simply planting seeds. You may not see the fruition of your intent or labor while you're physically alive, but your work goes on even after death. You have no idea the effect your smile had on the little boy in the grocery cart. Or the effect your gentle, respectful washing of the elderly man in the nursing home had on him the rest of his days. You may donate hours to youth ministry and never see a child turn a corner The day may come, however, when they reach a critical point in their lives, remember your conviction on truth and stay on the right course. You just don't know.

So what purpose does your living serve? You're part of The Plan, and it doesn't get any better than that. Live your life knowing that universe upon universe is witness to your existence. Nothing you do is lost. Reach for the highest and best in yourself and share it with others.

August 19, 2000

Everybody is a 'soul on a mission'

Do you ever think of yourself as a soul?

I have two all-time favorite movies. "Contact" and "Babe." When I'm in "the zone" at work I'm as happy as a clam at high tide, but you wouldn't know it to look at me. I am straight faced and determined, focused on things to do and places to go.

A co-worker remarked on my appearance a while back; she wasn't sure if I was angry or unhappy.

She stopped me in transit by laying a gentle hand on my arm. "Sally?" she inquired quietly, with care in her eyes. "Are you OK?"

I paused for a second, realizing how I must look to her. "I'm fine," I said with a smile.

A quote popped into my head, and I repeated it as I'd heard it so often, down to the tonal inflection and timing. "I'm just a pig on a mission!"

Her eyes widened and she choked out, "What?" I stepped over to my desk and picked up my stuffed Babe that I hugged on difficult days. I pressed a pink ear. "La la laaaa." Everyone in the office was laughing now. I pressed it again. "I'm just a pig..." obligingly emanated from my pet.

Each one of us is a soul on a mission. I know of those who know what their missions are. It doesn't necessarily make life easier. In some ways it is harder because if you have a momentary – or monumental – lapse in good judgment, your sense of failure can be tremendous.

But knowing the big picture of why you're here can open portals of wisdom and doors to action. You tend to trust your intuition more. You have a zeal for your mission that is undeniable. And it will call you, tell you, use whatever means necessary to influence you until you consciously adopt it or reject it. And you can reject it; you have the free will to do so.

But there is a price to pay, both as a human being alive on this planet and as your "essential self," a timeless soul in eternity.

If you thought of yourself as a "soul" (a spiritual being having a physical experience), what might you do differently? How might you look at the world? Seeing the world as a soul could pull you out of your daily humdrum routine and give you a wider perspective. It would change your priorities. You would experience more peace.

Ponder what your soul is, and how it happens that you are one. Most often, we think we HAVE one. And, of course, we take it on faith that a soul even exists. If it's real, it's invisible. Charity is invisible; can you hold it in your hand? It's an action we call charity, or kindness, or forgiveness. Just because souls can't quantitatively be measured doesn't mean they aren't real.

Thomas Moore, in "Care of the Soul" writes: "For the soul, it is important to be taken out of the rush (this is you) of practical life for the contemplation of timeless and eternal realities." Step back, step away; make some time to reflect and relish what you really are.

Many believe that when God breathed the breath of Itself into the dust and dirt, into nothingness, we became.

I choose to believe I am a soul. If I remembered that more often, I don't think I would get so bent out of shape over inconsequential things, like the bozo that cuts me off when the lane I'm in merges. And if I made a point of noting it often during the day, maybe I would be less concerned about my bank balance and feel more secure about life. Maybe I'd give the benefit of the doubt more often.

Maybe I wouldn't be so hard on myself and others. Maybe I'd devote more time in conscious "being" with my Creator.

Spend some time contemplating yourself as a spiritual being instead of a human being. It could inspire you to reach for greater things within yourself.

October 21, 2000

Beauty comes from within, not what society dictates

Nobody looking at me would wonder if I should be on the model's runway. No siree. I am a "giant economy size" middle-aged woman with thinning hair and glasses. Heaven forbid you would see me with my teeth out! I thought about going to work without them on Halloween, but I abandoned that idea; I didn't want to be the cause of an unauthorized work stoppage. Administration can be so picky about things like that.

No, I am not a classic beauty. And gauging from the sales of diet books, exercise videos and health supplements, a lot of other folks don't think they are either. Granted, many work out to improve their health. Still, they want to look "good." Our society frowns on the overweight, the aged, the impaired.

How is it that we allow others to influence us so deeply that we end up with less than optimal self-esteem? We give our power away by allowing our perspective to be governed by ad agencies. A person of my bearing would be queen material in another culture. But here, we put the young and the thin on a pedestal; may God catch you when you fall off.

There was a beautiful raven-haired 30-something movie star doing a hair color commercial a while back. While slow motion demonstrated the shine and thickness of her tresses, she commented on how it covered her gray so thoroughly.

'Skuse me? What's wrong with my gray? Why should I cover it? Now, I lighten my hair because it makes the bald spot on the back of my head less visible. The darker the hair, the more visible the scalp. The thing is, if you're going to color your hair, wear makeup, or have a tuck taken, do it because it makes YOU feel good. Not because "society" doesn't accept you for you for who and what you are.

Now see, right here I'm not walking my talk. I color my hair because it's embarrassing to have folks taller than me stand behind me and look down. And I know they're staring at my head because I can feel the air move when they adjust their tie or primp a curl in the mirror that is my scalp.

You are so much more than your crooked nose, wrinkles, or cellulite. Perhaps you're physically challenged; shorter or taller; fatter or thinner than the average. More than merely putting up with comments and stares, look at how what you're facing can make you empathetic to the situation of others. Can you pray for their strength and courage instead of judging and guessing why they are how they are? Can you just see them as another soul on a journey?

You're so much more than your physical being. If every child could be taught that they are precious sparks of God, souls created in the image of their Creator, we would have less violence and more compassion in the world. It's up to us to teach them that. Amen.

December 9, 2000

New opportunities come with each day

It seems like just yesterday we were partying like it was 1999. In a few days we'll be waking up in 01/01/01, and our lives will never be the same. Not because it's another year, but because every day is a new opportunity.

People have been expecting things from you since before you were born! Mama would pat her tummy and say you'll grow up to be the doctor in the family. Or Papa would pat Mama's tummy and say you'll be the next Elway or ARod. You could have been the most cherished or most rejected child ever. But the circumstances of your early years don't have to dictate the decisions and choices you make as an adult unless you let them.

A friend reports that she is being held accountable for the "feeling" in the office. Staff complained to her boss that if she comes in stressed or preoccupied, it sets the tone of the office and everybody has a stressful day. My friend says "These people aren't taking responsibility for their own behavior. So often I've gotten an earful of what son or husband has done. It doesn't change my day. I don't blame my disposition on them. We're not sheep or lemmings; we get to choose how we will react, say, and do".

Every moment of every day you have the freedom to change what you choose to believe, how you will behave, what you will think, who you will associate with. You get to choose whether or not to be happy, angry or sad. You may say "You can't poke me with a stick and not expect me to deck you!" Another may say "If you poke me with a stick I'm leaving". In this country, we get to choose. So choose what will serve you the best.

Each of us is a creation of God, of the highest order. We're sentient beings – able to think things through, weigh the pros and cons, and deliberate.

Don't give that power away! Don't "go along" just because its easier than standing up or thinking for yourself. I'm not saying you should poke the bully (boss, spouse, coworker, etc.) and not expect a reaction, but you do have the ability to think your way out of it.

Lots of folks need to have a demarcation point to make a significant change. For eons we've been using New Year's Resolutions for that purpose. Other's use birthdays or anniversaries. Whatever event you choose to use, consider making the decision to believe that your Creator didn't make a mistake when you were made.

You are precious! And if there isn't anyone to tell you that, know it as sure as you know you're breathing.

Your options every day are mind blowing! How can you not love and appreciate all that you are when you consider that the Creator of untold spiral universes made you, too!

Think outside the box for a change. Choose to see the good in everyone. Be all you can be, and encourage others to do the same. It's all within your reach.

2001

January 13, 2001

Self time line provides overview of life journey

Several years ago, I had an epiphany experience. That's when the light bulb goes on inside your head and suddenly you understand more completely, or an idea jells. They're such a revelation.

I am introspective. I like all kinds of mysteries. It is difficult for me to walk away from a puzzle of any sort. I like to know WHY.

I had been reading a book that advised making a time line of your life's events, then evaluating it from a dispassionate distance. So I did; it took weeks to construct and months to understand.

At first, I drew a line and wrote "born" at one end, and "40" at the other. Then I added major events, such as when my parents passed on, son was born, etc.

The big overview was done in a day. It stoked the memory fire and I added to it for weeks. This move, that move. This job, that job. Church events. Divorce. Friends.

One thing that emerged, as I look at "the big picture" and saw it in layers of meaning, was how often I had failed to carry out something I felt God had directed me to do.

I cannot adequately convey in words the depth of sadness that enveloped me as this realization settled in. I had let down the person I loved most. I get upset when my son doesn't send me a birthday card and look what I had – or hadn't – done.

In my dejected state came insight during prayer: Many ask God for guidance. That's what I did, and I got a response.

The response was that I had not failed. That being human, I can only see, say, from Point A to Point D. God wants me at Point G. I cannot conceive of Point G at all, so I can't be guided to it consciously. So I'm on my way, cruising past A and B, and at C, something breaks down. Something derails me and I don't reach that point.

I am not always aware that I have not reached a goal, but I am aware of a sense of being incomplete.

What I understood was that it was at those points, when I was at "C" that I was directed to "G" from there. I simply did not have the vision before that.

This could be your experience, too.

As we begin the new millennium, consider doing a time line. Ask God for guidance as you lay your life out in black and white.

Do you need to forgive yourself or another? Most of us do the best we can at any given time. Do you see any patterns of behavior that don't serve you? Maybe it's time to make some changes to increase your spiritual, physical, and emotional health. If it's your goal to be more compassionate, can you see how you could have done things differently and use them to guide you in the future?

Have faith and trust in yourself, and in God.

February 17, 2001

Break out of your box; explore

As you living your life by default or are you a conscious participant?

My word processing program didn't come set with the font and letter size I have now. I didn't even know I had a choice until I read the instructions.

Wow! I can express every mood and situation with a click of a mouse. It opened up vistas of expression I didn't know I had access to.

In my line of work, I use a lot of words. I create documents, banners, certificates, flyers and newsletters, all of which I use different specs for: I'm in heaven when I'm at my keyboard!

Growing up, my mother always bought white grapefruit and put salt on each segment. She said some folks put sugar on theirs, and others buy pink or red ones. But white with salt was best. So that's what I've always done. Until last year.

I've been on a grapefruit kick since October; just had a hankerin' for it. I eat one three or four times a week, at night, while watching TV.

In October I went to my favorite grocery store, only to find they didn't carry white grapefruit. Lots of pink and red, but no one. So I went to another store and they didn't carry them either. What's with this?

I tracked down an employee who told me white's aren't popular. Good heavens! Figuring I wasn't going to find them at any local store, I picked up a single pink and brought it home.

With trepidation, I sat to peel it that night. My mother's probably turning over in her grave, I thought. I'm a traitor to my upbringing.

I had taken off the material around a segment and thought about what a beautiful color it was. I popped it into my mouth and waited for the data to come in. Hmmm.... this is sweet, not puckery like a white; not as acidic. Hmmm... I put a little salt on one. Yech! It's better on its own. This is delicious!

One of the greatest lines of all time is "We've always done it this way." Don't fix what ain't broke" is another one. But somebody had to make a change in order to get to the methodologies they don't want to examine now.

You have one of the greatest minds in mankind. You are capable of tremendous creativity and imagination, of intuition and insight. Don't let "what is" keep you from exploring "what could be."

Give yourself permission to see your own potential. Just because you haven't always made the best choices for yourself doesn't mean you can't turn things around. Think outside the box. The "box" could be personal, family, or community expectations. Maybe you grew up with, "Oh, he'll never be anything but trouble," or "She's the tomboy in the family," and you accepted it.

We all have a God-given free will. You can change your course any time you want to, by the decisions you make. Live life consciously, not by default. You choose.

March 3, 2001

'Hannibal': Sinking below our humanness

As the last weekend in February closed out, receipts show that "Hannibal" was No. 1 at the box office for the third week in a row. People have shelled out more than ONE HUNDRED MILLION DOLLARS to see this movie.

What is the matter with this picture? What does it say about our society that movies such as this are so popular? How is it that we get a thrill seeing human beings being tortured, then gutted line animals on the Serengeti? The ads alone are alarming.

Have you seen it? Why did you want to see it? Was it because you like Anthony Hopkins as an actor? The cinematography?

You can get your fix elsewhere. Why would you subject your psyche to such violence?

Do you bemoan the quality of film the industry gives us, then validate its choices by going to see this type of brutality?

Do you consider yourself a decent, law-abiding citizen? Relatively high moral fiber? A religious person? Is this type of movie something you think Jesus, Buddha or Mahatma Gandhi would have enjoyed?

Or maybe you're just Joe and Jane Average. It probably didn't even occur to you that patronizing a film of this nature perpetuates its type.

Are you thinking, "Sally, you're overreacting. We've had flicks like this for ages and we're not cannibals. We're all OK."

Are we? Is our society "all OK?" Don't you see a connection between the steady diet of violence we feed ourselves, with the hate crimes and violence against others that is throughout our earth? Are our lives so devoid of excitement that we go in droves to see this dehumanizing junk?

Yes, we have had people actually do this abhorrent thing. Why do we need to glamorize it? It appeals to the lowest part of our humanness. Rise above, don't sink below.

Are you the same person who objects to their kids listening to Eminem's lyrics because they promote violence and offends your sense of right and wrong? There's a word for behavior like that.

If you crave vicarious violence, watch the news. You'll see exuberant people rioting in Pioneer Square tear-gassed and hit with rubber bullets, or observe a bus running down bystanders on a corner. That is reality.

People bleed and die. Children suffer. There are consequences in real life. But you don't see it on TV or the cinema.

Do you remember that old computer quote, "Garbage In / Garbage Out"? The quality of work done by the computer is equal only to the information put into it.

Every time we watch stuff that desensitizes us to awareness of each other, we hurt everyone because it wears down our level of tolerance.

In "Field of Dreams," we heard: "If you build it, they will come." But if they make it, it doesn't mean you have to go see it.

We need to be our own "spiritual police" and be vigilant about what we allow into our minds and bodies, our spirit and soul.

March 17, 2001

The power of reading is power of the spirit

You've probably heard by now that an entertainment industry writer's strike is on the horizon. And a couple airline ones, too. What do they have in common?

When you're sick of reruns, and while you're waiting for your flight, you can read. And I have some recommendations. These are all personal favorites that I own.

- If you want to go really, really deep, read "The Power of Now" by Eckhart Tolle. It is so thought provoking, a paragraph would frequently set me back on my heels for weeks. A life-changer. Excellent, but slow reading.
- In the mood for a devotional? The "Rekindling The Inner Fire" series, especially "Majestic Is Your Name" (St. Teresa of Avila), is a blessing. They're by David Hazard.
- Need something business related? I've given many copies of "Jesus as CEO," by Laurie Beth Jones, to friends.
- How about a coffee table book? "Illuminations of Hildegard of Bingen – Commentary by Matthew Fox" is on my top 10 list for content and beauty.
- "Meditation on the Word" by Dietrich Bonhoeffer continues to inspire all generations.
- For spiritual living, try "Conscious Union With God" by Joel Goldsmith and "Spiritual Literacy – Reading The Sacred In Everyday Life" by Frederic and Mary Ann Brussat.
- One of the most inspirational books I've ever read is "Your Life Is Your Message" by Eknath Easwaran. And it's true.
- A good book on women's studies is "The Feminine Face of God" by Sherry Ann Anderson.
- I have two favorites on mysticism (in a nutshell, mysticism is seeing God in everything). The first is "A Parenthesis In Time" by Joel Goldsmith and "The Mystic Vision" by Andrew Harvey.
- I spend a good deal of time doing dream work study and analysis. An excellent read is, "Wisdom of the Heart – Working With Women's Dreams" by Karen Signell.

I have a list of books I've told my son I hope he reads by the time he's 30. Several I've listed here already. We both have our favorite marked-up Bibles; that goes without saying.

Other books are:

- "St. George and The Dragon" by Fr. Edward Hays. Very good if you seek to understand the value of our life journey.
- "Naked Before God – The Return of the Broken Disciple," by Bill Williams. Wow... A must-read.
- "The Healing Light," by Agnes Sanford lifts you out of yourself.
- "Original Blessing," by Matthew Fox.
- "Building Your Field of Dreams," by Mary Manin Morrissey.
- "Breakthrough: Meister Eckhart's Creation Spirituality in New Translation," commentary by Matthew Fox.
- "Balancing Heaven and Earth," by Robert A. Johnson.
- My copy of "The Kingdom Within – The Inner Meaning of Jesus' Sayings," by John A. Sanford, is heavily underlined.

There are many good periodicals, too. I subscribe to "Spirituality and Health," a quarterly magazine, and "Science and Theology," a monthly newspaper. You can find them both on the Internet.

And while we're on "spiritual things," let's pray for rain.

April 28, 2001

'Lessons from the Dying' can be timely lessons for the living

Several weeks ago, Hospice of Kitsap County held a workshop titled, "Lessons from the Dying." Rodney Smith, author of a book by the same name, was the guest speaker. It was an enlightening, inspirational, three-hour, "too short" experience. A show of hands revealed that most of the participants were either involved with Hospice directly or were care providers.

I went because what I'd learned from my mother's passing transformed me, and I wanted to build on that.

A brochure outlined four goals:

- "Show the potential for spiritual growth at the end of life."
- "Identify the three most common spiritual lessons people address at the end of life."

- "Describe the optimum environment for a patient to learn and grow spiritually."
- "Identify techniques for caregivers and patients to utilize in creating this optimum environment for growth."

All of these goals were reached. A video of the workshop is available by calling Hospice of Kitsap County at (360) 415-6911.

There were stories of faith and fear, Peace and terror: I came away with two lessons learned.

The first was to be "present." It sounds easy, but give it some thought. When you're stacked up on I-5, tighter than pickles in a jar, where are your thoughts? When your daughter tells you she wants to be an exchange student anywhere, what's the first thing that comes to mind?

When I'm doing the dishes, I'm pretty much on autopilot. I'm thinking about what's left on my To Do list at work, what meetings are coming up, what I can send in the care package to my kid; anything but the dish, the soap and the water.

Everything has its own experience, however, and our minds must be retrained to pay attention to the "now."

The second lesson was the renewed emphasis that life is short and precious.

We truly don't know the day or time that our human form will case to be animated by God's "breath of life."

So many disagreements and judgments are over such stupid things. I recently caught myself getting worked up over where a box of materials was kept in my office. Was it worth stressing about? Absolutely not. But I was like a dog with a bone; I just wouldn't let go – until I realized I could choose not to let my emotions run over me. I recognized it as a matter of my will over someone else's, and I didn't need to win.

There is a book that recommends you live each day as though it were your last. Many issues and upsets that were important to you suddenly seem downright silly when you're looking at eternity. Do a life review and see where you can off-load some of the emotional and spiritual baggage you're carrying.

May 19, 2001

Life of Dalai Lama bears simple messages of reason, compassion

I was planning to write a column on the Dalai Lama's recent visit to Portland, so I contacted my editor to see if she knew of anyone going to see him. She didn't, so I accessed The Oregonian on the Web for its articles. Then I sat down with my copy of

"The Good Heart – The Buddhist Perspective of Jesus' Teachings," and started on my first draft.

The idea pops into my head to ask folks what their personal definition of compassion is, since it plays a central role in Buddhism. But work is hectic, and there's no chance to question anyone. A monthly noon meeting that is usually held in Port Orchard is moved to Silverdale. We lose half of the attendees and it ends early. I head over to Barney's to finish my article with a cup of coffee.

When I get there, I realize I have no money and take a table by the magazines instead of in the cafe. I read over what I've written thus far and psych myself into the piece. Out of the corner of my eye, I see a woman moving in my direction and our eyes connect. It feels like a flower has violently burst into bloom in my heart.

"Hi. I'm doing some research. Can I ask you a question?" Her whole demeanor glowed with happiness and tranquility.

"Of course. I hope I can be of help."

I asked her the question and a smile lit up her face. "From the Buddhist view..." she began, and forgive me, because I interrupted her.

"Ma'am, have you ever met the Dalai Lama?" I asked. Time seemed to stand still.

"I just came from the conference in Portland," she replied.

My jaw literally dropped and my eyes were big as dinner plates. "Please, do you have a few minutes to talk?"

I told her of the "coincidences" that led to our meeting. "Well, consider this," she said. "I live in Port Townsend. I stayed overnight at some friends in Gig Harbor last night, and just stopped by here to see if they had a book I'm looking for. You just got here and I'm getting ready to leave!"

Her name is Sheila Smith, and this is what she had to say.

"Even without using English, his body language radiates humor, humility, and strength of character. I have learned that how they (religious leaders) live their lives, not what they teach, is the best teaching.

What makes him a wonderful teacher is he really believes that reason and common sense are paramount," she continued. "If a lesson is in conflict with reason, go with reason. He encourages everyone to stay on the religious path they're already on, and be the best they can be within it. He bridges all faith and cultural barriers with his message of compassion, forgiveness, and non-violence; that's for everybody.

Our discussion ran on for some time, and at times we both cried. It was, we agreed, "a most fortuitous meeting."

If I had more space I could tell you more. But the message his life bears is ample food for thought.

June 16, 2001

Giving God human attributes
an injustice to the mystery

Wasn't it Tommy Smothers who coined the phrase, "Mom always loved you best"? Even though we laughed, it struck a chord with many people.

Sitting in the Mile Hill McDonalds in Port Orchard the other day (Mike Hoffman runs an excellent organization), I overheard twin daughters talking with their mom. The girls were about five years old; mom was busy tending a newborn.

"Mom", asked a pig-tailed beauty, "who do you like more?" Four eyes watched her intently. The mother turned and gave them a smile that would power California. This apparently answered the question because both tykes beamed back at her and went back to giggling and eating their lunch. They'd been through this before.

Most of us were taught to view God as a father. Does that equate to God being a human male? Yet we read in Genesis that male and female are made in God's image. That would seem to indicate that God is something else, something that combines these energies, not merely one or the other. Do you agree that God is not a human being, not corporeal? Then what is God? As Mr. Spock would say, "Pure energy"?

God has often been portrayed as an unforgiving, uncompassionate parent. Any child who has cringed at the thought of father coming home and the physical, emotional and verbal abuse that ensued may have a hard time relating to "Abba", Jesus' "Daddy": emotionally present, always supportive, encouraging and fair.

Even folks who have made the transition from the God of the Hebrew Bible (Old Testament) to "Abba" can have difficulty understanding why the reference to God as man was made. It takes going to the original languages, studying the times, the political climate and the patriarchal investment.

While referring to God as a parent helps us to relate to an invisible power (can you seriously be held accountable for your thoughts and actions by something called "Energy"?), putting God into human form and giving It human attributes does the Maker of the abyss and Creator of black holes a serious injustice.

Human beings are fickle creatures, tossed about by hormones, experiences and biases. Surely the Creator is beyond any descriptions our little minds can conceive of.

If we agree that we don't have a handle on God (I think God is beyond our full and complete comprehension. Otherwise, we'd be God too, and you know what the Bible said about THAT!), then why do we continue to place females in subordinate positions in many of our churches and, by extension, our communities? Listen to what is being preached, sung and taught without coming right out and saying it. Do you limit yourself to Mother's Day references of God as a chicken guarding her eggs? We still have churches that teach that females are lower (some say equal but different) in God's eyes than males are, which has propagated domestic violence and a woman's lower self-esteem.

God is a mystery that we try to get a handle on. But if we did, God wouldn't be God.

July 28, 2001

Talk to God,
and you might be surprised by her answers

Imagine a different kind of "Conversation With God."

"Hi Mom, it's me – just checking in."

"Hello honey! It's so good to hear from you. So tell me – what's going on in your life? Not like I don't know already, but I like to hear the sound of your voice."

Sitting in my truck at the boat launch in Port Orchard, I was watching this gorgeous champagne colored SUV deposit a Bayliner of the same shade in the water.

"Ma," I said, "I'm enjoying today's cooler weather. The sunrise was absolutely breathtaking and my neighbor's flowers have bloomed. I'm a happy camper."

A couple were off-loading a pair kayaks from the top of their car.

"The mosquito's are eating me alive at night" I whined. "They're having a field day on my cholesterol. Can't you do something about it?"

God's laugh could be heard to the ends of the earth. "Oh, absolutely. I'll alter the balance of nature just for you!"

"Gee, Ma, you don't have to be so sarcastic!" We both giggled hard as I swatted one away.

"So," said Mom slowly, "how's your identity crisis coming along?"

I paused while pitching old popcorn out to a pair of seagulls.

"You're right, of course. That is my experience right now" I began. "There is some comfort in labels people give you because they precede you and pave the way. For example, am I Republican or Democrat? Since I vote the issue and the person, I can't say I'm either. Am I Mormon, Methodist or Jewish? Since I believe religion is an expression of you, I don't feel comfortable being one over the other." I laid my head against the back of my seat and stared at the visor. "All I really know about me is that I'm a human female; middle aged, to boot. With health issues." A couple crows joined the gulls, jockeying for position outside my door. I watched in silence for a while.

"What about me?" came the gentle question.

Immediately I teared up. "That's the crux of things, isn't it?" I closed my eyes and took a couple of deep breaths. The cool, marine air was deeply comforting and I allowed the swell of emotion to pass. "I know that you aren't male or female. That it's easier to communicate with you as if you were when I need to think. But I also believe that you and I aren't "you and I." That on some cosmic level, we're all one. That would mean I'm here talking to myself."

"Should I get the net?" Mother asked, a smile in her voice. "I'm serious" I pushed on. "When I ponder that a spark of divinity is in me, it encourages me to try harder, do better. When I think that God and I are one, I don't see as many limitations. I make better choices. It makes me a better person."

God put her hand out to touch me and it felt like a ray of sunlight.

"I love you, Mom."

"And I love you, Precious."

August 11, 2001

To get lowdown on God, look around (or in mirror)

The years I spent in youth ministry are some of my fondest. I loved every kid we had, even the "pickles." Each one had something to learn, and something to teach the rest of us.

Being an adult in youth ministry meant you spent some time in the church van picking them up or taking them home. Usually the kids would gather into groups and chat on the way in to church. On the way home, however, we usually sang.

A couple weeks ago I was watching TV and this particular episode of "Mysterious Ways" ended with Joan Osborne singing "One Of Us." Immediately I went back in time to the van with the kids, and we were all singing our lungs out. "What if God was one of us? Just a slob like one of us. Just a stranger on the bus trying to make his way home." Every time that song came on the radio, talking ceased and we belted it out.

"What if God was one of us?"

In Matthew 25 we read that we are to clothe the naked, feed the hungry, visit the sick and imprisoned because "when you do it to the least of my brethren, you do it to me." Sounds to me like God IS one of us. And it's us!

"That's blasphemy!" you say, as you line the birdcage with my face. But look at this line, "...when you do it to the least of my brethren, you do it to me." How we can gloss over this one! If you honestly believed this was true, what would you do differently? It can be near impossible to see God in the face of the person who took a life, or abused a child, or sold meth. And yet we are directed to "Love God with all you are and your neighbor as yourself."

We so under utilize the God spark within us.

Often we hear ourselves referred to as "a child of God." If you know this to be true in the center of your being, are you living the life it brings with it? And what does that make you? If you were the offspring of a king or queen, wouldn't that make you royalty, even if you no longer had a kingdom and were flat broke? Circumstances don't change your lineage. In the immortal words of Popeye, "I yam what I yam."

God is not "out there." God is "in here." When you create a vase on the pottery wheel, compose music or arrange words, God is there. Nothing exists, not person, plant, protozoa or pine tree, without God. Not rocks or rivers, super nova or sperm whale. Nothing in creation exists outside of the Creator.

I have a six-year-old friend who blows my mind with her wit, intellect and nerve. She can really be a "pickle!" I say to her, "Oh, Kady, please use your powers for good!" She laughs like she knows what I'm talking about, and somewhere inside all of us, we remember we're made of stardust!

August 18, 2001

Give thanks, and this time, mean it

Most Sundays at 9 a.m. I'm in my living room with a cup of coffee, watching "Life Keys" with Rev. Mary Manin Morrissey on channel 22. Once in a while something is said that causes me concern (only because it isn't a part of my present belief structure), but I'd have to say that 95% of the time what she teaches is right on, at least to my way of thinking. There is usually what we could acknowledge as a point of agreement or kernel of truth in all faith systems or religions. Even those we would consider the most violent of our age profess to love God. And they do, according to their faith.

Her denomination is called New Thought, and while its teachings and philosophy certainly contribute to what she says, it's not the denomination that draws me. It's her heart, her words, her integrity and honesty. Her website is at www.lecworld.org. On a recent Sunday, the topic was gratitude. There have been books on it in recent years, it's been featured on talk shows, and while I totally agreed with what was said, I didn't keep up with the recommended paperwork associated with it. My "Gratitude Journal" was left sitting at the kitchen table as I rushed off hither and yon. I had found myself repeating the same things I was grateful for day after day. What's the purpose of that? I know I'm grateful! But on this day, she said to write down the first 10 things that came to mind. Then, every day for the next 39 days, you write down one item in the morning and one in the evening, without duplicating yourself. That shouldn't be too difficult, I thought. I'm still working on it.

What is the value in being grateful? What good is there in cultivating an "attitude of gratitude?"

Mystics through the ages have had this attitude. I think it's an indicator of an individual's acceptance of their divine spark. How can you look up at night into a clear sky and not marvel at the twinkly stars and planets fixed in space by an unseen hand? How can you look at the food that nourishes you and not thank the plant or creature that is giving you its energy? And who has not had a major project deadline at work and failed to thank the machine that made the copies without requiring the KeyOp?

Being grateful for literally everything in your life, even the "bad stuff," opens your heart to see the good in everything. "All things work together for good to those that love and serve God," states Romans 8:28. Not some things. All things.

Author Sarah Ban Breathnach writes, "Both abundance and lack exist simultaneously in our lives, as parallel realities. It is always our conscious choice which secret garden we will tend." Consciously choose to recognize the bounty you have, no matter how small. The attention you give it will bless your life.

August 25, 2001

Freeing ourselves to consider what we were meant to be

I felt like Linda Blair in "The Exorcist" as I backed out of my spot in the grocery store parking lot recently. With my head swiveling around, trying to make sure there were no approaching vehicles or pedestrians from any direction, I cautiously inched my way out.

Wouldn't it be wonderful if all of life's threats were that easy to see? So often they are invisible yet no less threatening, like some thoughts and attitudes. If they came blazing before us with warning labels attached, such as "Dwelling on 'what ifs' is hazardous to your health," you could see them for what they are and choose to think something else. Unless we catch ourselves, though, we can be at the mercy of our own minds!

A threat could be defined as something that keeps you from reaching your God-given potential. Eating more than a couple Oreo's at a time is a threat to good health, as is dwelling on the past. Whether the memories are positive or negative, long term avoidance of the here and now will not make a better tomorrow.

Backing out of my spot in the parking lot, I was hoping there was nothing in my "blind side"- the little area where you can't see no matter how many mirrors you have. What's over there, an SUV? Will I survive the impact? Will my air bags deploy and Lord, they're expensive to replace! Threats are everywhere but never more threatening than when we're so used to them we don't listen to them anymore, or ignore them.

Allowing ourselves to become desensitized to human suffering is a threat to us in many ways. A friend of mine is hooked on WWF wrestling. "It's all choreographed; nobody's seriously hurt," he says. I tried to watch but I just couldn't. I felt agitated and distressed. "Why are you watching this? What do you get out of it?" I asked. "It's fun," he said. "But why? Why is brutality so fun?" "I can't explain it," he responded. So many movies and games glorify violence. They take away the consequences and stress the adrenalin rush.

Physician and author Andrew Weil advocates putting yourself on a diet of no TV news for a time because the news is mostly bad news: murders, fires, uprisings, bank robberies, etc. All things that raise your cortisol (fight or flight hormone) level and can, over time, lower your immune system function.

What you think, what you watch, what you put in your mind is of incredible importance. Every thought has a chemical counterpart. You've heard of the "runner's high"- endorphins released at a certain point create a feeling of euphoria. Fear creates cortisol; sadness and ambivalence, frustration and desire all have their own signature chemicals. Two excellent authors on this subject are Dr. Candace Pert and Caroline Myss. Myss will be in Seattle in October; she's an outstanding presenter. When you accept that you consciously choose your thinking and behavior, you decrease the "threats" in your life, and become more of the person you were meant to be.

September 22, 2001

Words fail at tragic time like this, but faith won't

It is often difficult, in the 500 words I'm allotted per column, to express what I'm trying to convey as thoroughly as possible. Today, it's almost impossible. What we have experienced will change all of us forever.

What has it brought out in you? Many have volunteered their resources and attended community services to mourn and show solidarity.
What did it bring out in me?

I was numb watching TV at work on Tuesday. Most of us were incapable of stringing thoughts together at that time. It was just incomprehensible, in the same way that Oklahoma City was. I had a doctor's appointment later that morning that my son took me to. I can't drive now, due to my cataracts, so we were together in his car when I had this overwhelming need to pray. In the parking lot of the clinic we held hands and opened our hearts.

"Father/Mother/God, so many of your sons and daughters have lost their earthly lives and may be unable to recognize or accept what has just happened to them. We join our prayers with others, Lord, in asking that you send your angels to guide them to the Light. Dear God, they have not had time to prepare their hearts or minds to leave the earth, and may not know to go to the Light. As we pray we know this is being done. Thank you, our Blessed Creator."

Those who have passed over are in the arms of God now. We are still here, dealing with the after effects of tremendous loss. Many have written and spoken on what we can and should do to help our children and ourselves return to normalcy in the midst of intense grief and outrage. It will take time.

I add my voice to those who do not paint all our brothers and sisters of Middle Eastern descent with the same brush. A handful of individuals committed these acts. If a group of Americans bombed a European landmark, we would not want them to attempt to destroy the United States in retaliation.

I think the most powerful thing we can do is pray. Pray for those who have passed over, for those who face the carnage every day in the recovery effort. Pray for those who lost their loved ones, lost their jobs and businesses. Pray for strength, for the will to forgive.

St. Francis wrote, "Lord, make me an instrument of thy peace. Where there is hatred, let me sow love; where there is injury, pardon; where there is doubt, faith; where there is despair, hope; where there is darkness, light; and where there is sadness, joy. O divine Master, grant that I may not so much seek to be consoled as to console; to be understood as to understand; to be loved as to love.

For it is in giving that we receive; in pardoning that we are pardoned; and in dying to self that we are born to eternal life." Amen.

October 6, 2001

Let respect, love for God remain

It has been several weeks since the September 11th tragedy. Leaders are advising that we resume our previous routines for many reasons: the economy needs to be maintained, and our psyches need respite from the tremendous emotional turmoil. Do you think the terrorists planned that date on purpose? 9-1-1.

While it is imperative that we not give terror a victory by abdicating our essential way of life, there are a few things we do now that we didn't do so much of then that we should keep on doing.

Before this happened, a hero was someone who received millions for playing a game, or someone in a video that destroyed everything. A hero was a pop star in a tube top.

Today our hero's are moms and dads who took their kids to school and practice. They're service workers who risk their lives everyday because of the high-risk nature of their work on behalf of others. A hero is a child who brightened the lives of all they knew with their smile and love for life. The neat thing is, they're with us everyday; we just need to recognize them. When you see your neighbor at school, work or church, be aware that you're in the presence of greatness and treat them with respect.

Before 9-1-1, our political system was fractured. We have two basic parties who do their best to represent those that vote for them, but often times the process is polluted with ego issues and stubbornness. We have shown that we can come together and work for the greater good when we want to. The lions have lain down with the lambs, and both got what they wanted.

Before 9-1-1, there were those that had God neatly packaged, tucked away for special occasions. Now they're hanging on to God for dear life. Exactly! For "dear life." Because life IS dear, and to paraphrase an old soda commercial, "Things go better with God." If there is only one thing that remains from the overwhelming pain that erupted on that date, let it be that our appreciation and love for God, our devotion to each other's well being, remains. For to love God is to love each other.

Right now, our emotional "rubber band" is pulled wide, not unlike the feeling we have when we're first "in love." But it isn't healthy to sustain it; feel the tension as you hold it open. Eventually we'll lose that sense of expansiveness and resume our normal "shape." And when we do, I'm hoping we will have made some changes that remain when the band snaps back.

Right now we're doing a good job of living The Golden Rule. Let us consciously decide to continue being courteous. Let us avoid jumping to conclusions and assuming the worst in each other. Let us praise our Creator for the good to be found in this disaster. And may our lives be a living prayer "without ceasing."

October 27, 2001

"He Really Gave Us A Cross To Bear This Time; How Are You Doing?"

This month I've faced two surgeries, a back injury, dead computer, death in our work family, and a few other things that made these last few weeks very difficult. I do so much better with "good stress" than "bad stress," don't you? Lord knows, we've felt a lot of the "bad stress" lately.

I was watching "Religion and Ethics" on Channel 9 at 5 a.m. last Sunday when psychotherapist Rev. Joan Kavanaugh of Riverside Church in New York was interviewed. Asked what the overall theme was of those coming to her in the wake of 9-11, she said that most of her clients were wondering how God could allow "this" to happen to them. They were decent people, law-abiding citizens. Why didn't God protect them? "What was your response?" asked the moderator. "That we have a God who is with us in terrible things but who does not protect us," she answered. "That it has to be a journey and a deepening maturity of our religious faith."

Lutheran pastor/religious historian Dr. Martin Marty also was interviewed. When asked, "How can Americans deal with constant anxiety?" he had several responses. One I found illuminating (go to www.pbs.org for the full interview) was, "The first thing one does is to put the right name on things." Are you really afraid that a plane will fly into the building you work in? Are you really afraid that you'll come in contact with anthrax? If you were to put the "right name on" your fear, wouldn't it be fear of death or dying?

Unlike events that devastate us then fade to allow for healing, the scab on this wound keeps getting picked off. We're told to prepare psychologically for a war that may go on for years. How do you do that? That we should be prepared for body bags coming in from around the world, and continued acts of terrorism in our own country. The wound will become infected if it isn't cleaned up and allowed to repair itself.

How can you protect yourself and your family from the on-coming emotional onslaught? This list reflects some things that can assist you.

- Limit the amount of news you absorb every day.
- You don't know if anything is going to happen to you so don't manufacture scenarios that promote heartburn. Take reasonable precautions. If something happens, it happens.
- Devote at least as much time to reading/listening uplifting, hopeful materials as you do taking in sorrowful, frightening stuff.
- Read Job; pray for discernment. Pray for the perpetrators as well as the victims.

If you find that you are doing OK emotionally, find ways to help others de-escalate their anxiety. One of the best things you can do is, by your actions and words, let others know that you have a peace that passes all understanding and that it comes from faith in the Creator of all that is seen and unseen. All things, not some things, work together for good for those that love God.

November 3, 2001

Any day's a good day to find God, tragedy or not

We're hearing from across the nation that there is a surge in church attendance; that people are praying more than before. A televised report on a church in New York near Ground Zero reported that confessions were up 300% since 9-11, and that services were scheduled to accommodate grave, day and swing shifts.

Many people associate God with a building. Or they only turn to God in times of devastation and disaster, or because all of a sudden they're afraid of dying with sin in their souls. Turning to God only because of fear of the hereafter is to miss the total and absolute joy of being embraced by unconditional love in the here-and-now. My hope is that these churches, now with captive audiences, take this opportunity to each these wonderful people about the love of God; about how God is there wherever they are at all times; about how they have a spark of God within them and can fan it into fire. God is as near to us as our heartbeat, but many have been taught that God is like an absentee landlord – he only comes around when he wants something, or when something broken needs fixing. I believe in a God that lives in my house with me; makes my favorite chicken and eggplant stir-fry with me; pays my extensive medical bills for me - sometimes with the help of human angels.

We absolutely do not need to have organized prayer in schools. Kids, teachers, custodians and support staff, have probably been praying 24/7 since 9-11. Christians, Buddhists, Muslims – people of all faiths may communicate with their Creator at different, or at all times. You can be in as close a connection in a garden as a church; on the football field as in a surgical suite. In a place of worship you have the advantage of corporate prayer, of meeting with like-minded people who can support your journey in faith, and the structure to provide for religious training. God is everywhere, in all situations and events. Christians are advised to "pray without ceasing." How do you think that is accomplished? How different would your life be if you gave the Creator of the cosmos an "all access pass" to your mind, heart and spirit? What's stopping you?

If you're one of those folks who thinks that now is a good time to reacquaint yourself with God - just in case - let me tell you something I have come to believe. God really is love. That may not have been your experience growing up, but there are a lot of theories about God out there and you don't have to be stuck with the one you have now if it doesn't work for you. If it doesn't help you grow in compassion, forgiveness and joy for yourself and others; if it doesn't lead to a life of service, surrender and faith in God's love for you.

Take that first step. Find a quiet place conducive to reflection, and ask God for guidance and wisdom. God will not fail you.

December 8, 2001

"Make 'New Reality' A Better One

It has been difficult for me to keep from crying tears of joy every day since the patch was taken off my second eye following cataract surgery on Nov. 26. Having both eyes now with new lenses has proven to be a metaphor for life as well. Seeing clearly and cleanly without living in a literal yellow fog has opened me up to see the world in a different light. I feel like I'm in a "new reality."

You've heard that term many times since 9-11. Folks with their routines of activity and thinking disrupted have longed for a return to "business as usual." We're told now that life, with its emphasis on heightened awareness of security, circumstances and surroundings, is our "new reality."

Years ago, in an effort to make sense of some experiences, I came up with the following life theory.

Perhaps you, too, have been through periods of tremendous upheaval when logic seems suspended and you're getting along not one day at a time, but one minute at a time. When your prayers come from a place of so much pain, you can barely breathe. When it's hard to remember why you put your shoes on. For some reason, I came to associate this period of time as life with the clutch pushed to the floor. The vehicle (me) is still moving but isn't "under power." The gears (goals) that normally propel me along are disengaged. It doesn't happen often, but I've learned that this is a window of opportunity that can herald a "new reality" for me. Being thoroughly separated from the ordinary, I am now open to integrate some deep "course corrections" into my daily living. As author James Hillman writes, "You have to give up the life you have to get the life that's waiting for you."

I believe that we, as a nation, are in such a time right now; are facing an incredible opportunity to make some powerful, deep changes in our thinking and behaviors precisely because we've been shaken to our roots.

As a whole, before 9/11 we took a lot for granted: our safety as a nation, the presence of our loved ones, our jobs and our relationship with our Creator. We floated along fairly complacently in the little cocoon we'd knitted around ourselves, insulated by our personal concerns. Suddenly, "their" pain is our pain. "Their" loss is our loss. We open hearts, check books, tears gush and we're all pulling together. And then... inevitably...the rubber band that was stretched thin begins to pull back. We begin the process of letting the clutch up from the floor to settle in to the old gear. Please, don't let that happen.

Take advantage of this extraordinary opportunity to review your life. Ask yourself, "How can I be a better lover of myself, my family, my community and my God?" Think of those that didn't get to go home on September 11th. Decide how you'll improve your life. Pray for strength, then do it.

December 29, 2001

Trust God to bring a good year

She sat alone in her old Plymouth at the end of Trenton Ave., absorbing the view from Bachman Park. Engine running to provide some heat on this cold morning, she watched the seagulls soar around the ferry that was on its way out of town.

"I used to have some place to be on December 31st," she thought to herself. But now, with her husband and kids gone, she looked forward to her bottle of sparkling cider and bed after the 10 o'clock news. It would be the same day tomorrow as today, for as far into the future as God allowed. God… "I wonder what He does on New Year's Eve?" crossed her mind.

"I'm with anyone who wants to be with me," came the reply from the gentleman wrapped in a warm coat that sat next to her. As hard as she tried to remember later, she couldn't find a reason why she didn't jump out of her skin. "You're…" she began. He smiled. "I'm the image of what you imagine God to look like, is that correct?" "I, ah, well, yes, I do believe so," she said. It was the God from her childhood: an old man with a white beard, not unlike Santa Claus. "Why are you here with me, of all people, out here in the cold?" "You wondered what I do on New Year's Eve, right? And I said I'm with anyone who wants to be with me. Just as I am every split nanosecond of every moment of every hour of every day. Back to New Years… you used to throw quite the parties," said God. She nodded her head. "That was when my husband was alive and the kids were young. Everyone is gone now and my house is quiet." Her head dipped down and she felt tears well up. "I miss them all. I miss their smiles, the laughter. I miss the busy-ness of friends, especially this time of year. I feel empty." Tears rolled off her cheeks and fell onto the faux fur of her winter coat.

He handed her a tissue. "I know what that empty feeling is like," said God. "So many of my kids don't check in with me, either. You set them out on the path of life and with free will, they pretty much do what they want. Even if you warn them about the pitfalls and give them all the love they can take, it doesn't always guarantee smooth sailing." They sat in companionable silence for a minute, remembering times past.

"So how does God celebrate the New Year?" she asked as she wiped her nose. He smiled broadly and said, "I make goals just like everyone else. I've got a couple big ones this year, too." The car was toasty warm now and she had warmed up to this visitor. "Can you tell me what your plans are?" His eyes twinkled with happiness. "Every age my offspring grow in their ability to understand more of their Old Man. Through the centuries I've seen them spend more time trying to understand why things are the way they are. And they're finally 'getting' that their choices in the midst of what they consider to be 'trying times' makes all the difference. They're a chip off the old block so I've given them a lot of power they're just learning to utilize. Life isn't 'done unto' them, they decide how they'll respond. I've got a couple souls in place that will help them move into this, and it's an opportunity that will change the earth. I can hardly wait to see what will happen! And the second one is special, just for you." Startled, her eyes opened wide. "M-me?" she stammered. "You thought of me, specifically?" "I'm here with you now, right?"

She closed her eyes tightly, wishing she'd spent more time in God's presence over the years, when she heard a knock on her window. Opening her eyes she glanced over quickly to the now empty passenger side. Turning her face to the window she saw a large passenger van full of seniors in the parking lot, smiling and chatting as they disembarked. She rolled down her window after seeing the smile of the woman who had knocked. "We're from out-of-town and were wondering if you could tell us about this wonderful place," she sparkled. Shutting off the car, she exited her old Plymouth to celebrate the New Year in a new way. This was God's surprise for her, she knew; a new life, with new choices and new friends.

2002

January 5, 2002

Books on this list you can take to heart, soul

Back by popular demand is my list of recommended reading, updated for 2002. I've divided this list into books I've read (I wasn't able to read much through September), books I'm reading now, and those I'll be reading later this year.

BOOKS I'VE READ

1. If I was Oprah, I'd put Edward Hayes' "St. George and the Dragon" under everyone's chair. I re-read it this year with a magnifying glass. I'm going to devote a column to this book later in the year. See all his work at www.forestof-peace.com. Also, he's featured at www.spiritualityhealth.com in their "Living Spiritual Teachers" section.

2. "The Four Agreements" by Don Miguel Ruiz. There was no doubt for me after studying them that they were right on: "Be impeccable with your word," "Don't take anything personally," "Don't make assumptions," and "Always do your best." These can be tough to live out! The companion book is also wonderful.

BOOKS I'M READING

1. "Sacred Contracts" by Caroline Myss. I have read all her previous works, listened to a lot of tapes, and understood in my head what she was stating. There's that old saying that when the student is ready the teacher appears. I cried reading just the introduction of this book; all the pieces started coming together for me. I'll see her at her book signing in Seattle on January 23rd at EastWest Books.

2. "Practicing The Power of Now" by Eckhart Tolle. The "Power of Now" took me a long time to get through, but it was worth it; what I learned is a part of how I consciously live. His new book, however, serves to facilitate what it teaches by providing exercises and meditations.

3. "There's a Spiritual Solution to Every Problem" by Wayne Dyer is excellent. I have questions that I'd like to ask all these writers on how they'd apply their understandings to specific situations. For example, they don't address the lives of children often, if at all, and I'm hoping to see that as I progress in this book.

BOOKS I'LL READ

1. Mary Manin Morrissey (my favorite spiritual director) has a new book out titled "Nothing Less than Greatness," which deals with relationships. I feel led to read specific books at specific times. This one will be running alongside "Sacred Contracts" soon.

2. Coming out in January is James Redfield's "God and The Evolving Universe." I learned so much from "The Celestine Prophecy"; I can't wait to read this one.
3. "The Heart of the Soul" by Gary Zukav is sitting on my couch. Just looking at it, my heart rate settles down and I feel peaceful. Have you ever seen him on TV? He exudes depth and calm.
4. I'm on the waiting list at the library for "The Open Heart" by HH The Dalai Lama. Friend Asha says it will help me with some challenges I'm facing now.

Due to space limitations I can't get everything in, but this should give you some good ideas. Happy New Year!

February 16, 2002

Don't lose your way; just turn on the light

Almost everyone has had the experience of walking into a dark, unfamiliar room and stubbing a toe or worse on something hard. You feel out of your element, your anxiety level is heightened because you don't know what to expect, and you've lost track of time. You can't find your way and you don't know where you're going. It's disorienting and you feel vulnerable. Fear creeps in because you don't know what's there that could hurt you.

If only you could turn on the Light.

For many, life is like living without illumination. You go through the motions of your day without having a real sense of purpose. You stumble around, hoping to find some meaning for your existence. Even people who have faith in God ask themselves this.

I had a conversation recently with a man who was struggling to know why he was alive; it wasn't enough to know God had created him. Why, exactly, was he here? Was it just to suffer, he asked, or to raise his kids? If someone were to ask you: "Why are you here?" what would you say?

Growing up as a Roman Catholic, I was told in my Confirmation class that my purpose in life was to "know, love and serve God in this world and the next." I took that literally as a kid and still choose to live by that statement. But not everyone has something that definitive to guide their lives with.

If you think you're missing something; if you feel there should be something more to life, then consider turning on the Light. The electricity is always there – its up to you to put the plug into the outlet. We were created with free will. God issues everyone an invitation to connect with the power source – Itself – over and over.

How often have you felt overwhelmed by the beauty of our area? Or held a newborn and marveled at the tiny toes and button nose? Or felt proud of yourself because you stopped smoking? All of these events and so many more are open doors to connecting with God. And if you grew up with the belief that God is a harsh, loveless deity (so there's no way you'd even want to know God anyway!), there are many people who can testify otherwise. God is worth bringing into your life.

I collect quotes, primarily on spirituality, leadership, gratitude, forgiveness and others. My favorite by far is from Socrates: "The unexamined life isn't worth living." If you aren't sure your life is worth living as it is right now, take the risk and ask God to reveal Itself to you (I use the word "Itself" because God is neither male or female.) If you already know, love and serve God, ask to go to the next level of commitment and relationship.

God is the Light that illuminates the universe. Choose to move away from the darkness and toward the Light. All you have to do is ask.

March 2, 2002

As lifetimes go, today is all that matters

Mortality: It's not that I fear where I'm going, it's the process that gets me there that has my attention.

Most of us can't predict when our souls will return to the Creator. It could be during an accident on the highway, or on a flight, or because our bodily functions decide not to anymore. But someday, our physical life will cease to be and we will return to the form of existence we came from; at least, that is my belief.

I was reading an article on Waylon Jenning's crossing over due to complications from diabetes the other day. The article stated he had difficulty walking prior to having a foot removed. I have difficulty walking now because of this, and my father, also diabetic, had seven amputations before he passed on. As I sit here at my computer, barely able to see through my tears, so utterly aware of my humanness, my disease, my life, I ask myself, "What is most important for me to complete, or do, or be in this life? What contributions are most important for me to make? If its true that all you take with you when you die is your knowledge and love, how can I be more loving now? What can I do to make life better for those I care about? What injustices can I right? Am I walking my talk?"

There is no better time than this very moment to fully live your life. Identify what is most important to you and "make it so." Don't put off hugging your child, or saying thank you, or taking time to admire the trees or a butterfly. Look at your life as though you only had one more week on earth, and review your priorities through that lens.

If you knew your time to leave was near, who would you want to apologize to, or forgive? Whose forgiveness would you seek? Do it now. What letters would you write or phone calls would you make? Do you have an up-to-date will (having this done will spare your loved ones the pain and anxiety of having to deal with this)? Do it now. Are there words you regret saying? Do you need to reconcile with anyone? There's no better time than the present. When's the last time you told your friends and family how much they mean to you, and how grateful you are for their love and support? Do it now and do it often.

And speaking of the present, "be" present. Don't spend your precious time rehashing old grievances or failures; what good does that do? It just makes the acid in your stomach and your stress level rise. Why waste your precious time getting your "underwear in a knot" over something of no serious value, like who left the top off the toothpaste? What on earth does this have to do with eternity?

This is the day God has made for us; let us rejoice and be glad in it!

March 30, 2002

Never forget that, like Jesus, you, too, can forgive

"Father, forgive them – they don't know what they're doing."
These, we are told, are the last words of Jesus before he died over two thousand years ago. So much has been written about these words. Have you ever meditated on them? Allowed them to percolate inside you?

When doing "dream work", one method of learning its meaning is to diagram it out. You write out all aspects of the dream as completely and thoroughly as you can, recalling as many details (such as night or day, rain or shine, color or lack thereof) as possible. Then you take little pieces of it, such as "It was a dark and stormy night…" and write out what it means for you. The meaning usually becomes clear quickly. Sometimes its confirmation of a perception or it helps you understand why you responded the way you did. I can honestly say that there was a point in time where understanding the meaning in a series of dreams literally saved my life.

Let's look at Jesus' words in this way.

"Father, forgive them…"

I'm not sure there are any more important words written anywhere. For me, these are right up there with "Love God with your whole heart, soul, mind and strength, and your neighbor as yourself."

Here we have a man (whether you believe he is the son of God or not, depending on your faith) who, through no obvious fault of his own, is publicly humiliated, abandoned by his friends, and killed. Nailed through his hands and feet to roughly hewn bars of wood and left to die for all to see. No closing of a curtain to keep voyeuristic eyes away; no concern for him at all.

We often gloss over the humanity of Jesus, as if his "divinity" somehow exempted him from suffering. Here was a human being, in the flesh, just like you and me. Tortured in both body and spirit ("Father, please let this cup pass from me", i.e. "I don't want to do this if I don't have to"), he suffered extraordinarily for what he believed in. Why on earth would he then ask God, his and our Creator, to forgive those who had done this to him?

"Father, forgive them…" What is there that you need to forgive someone for? Forgiveness heals all parties.

"… - they don't know what they're doing."

I've never thought this just meant that the people didn't know they were killing the one and only son of God. For if we truly "got" that we are all offspring of the one Creator, no matter our religious affiliation or nationality, how could we take anyone's life, anywhere, at any time? Wouldn't we work harder to find resolutions that didn't shed blood?

If there is anything for any individual to take from Easter, whether you consider yourself a Christian or not; no matter your faith or beliefs, its that God loves you unconditionally. And as we've seen with Jesus, the people who abused him and took his life didn't ask God to forgive them – he did for them. You have the strength to forgive.

April 13, 2002

Make sure you don't miss the message in today's hectic world

I'm not always the sharpest tack in the box.

I escorted a meter reader to our locked electrical box recently at work, my mind back at my desk in the project I was engrossed in. The gentleman, very upbeat and cheerful, completed his task and turned to walk back to his truck. I had just opened the door to re-enter the building when he said, "Take care!" To which I responded, "You're welcome!"

The door closed behind me and I slapped the palm of my hand on my forehead in a classic "I coulda had a V-8" moment as I realized what I had just done.

This event was a lesson for me in two ways:

- I wasn't "present." I was there physically but not mentally. I missed out on fully enjoying the benefit of this persons engaging smile and personality because I was not in the "now."
- I wasn't "listening." Often we catch ourselves responding to what we "think" we heard or saw because we anticipated it. I must have assumed he was going

to say, "Thank you", because "You're welcome" certainly was not the appropriate response. I expected to hear one thing, and it was much more.

Our relationship with our Creator is often like the above.

The beauty and "personality" of God is all around us, yet we often miss it because we aren't "present."

It was taking me longer to fall asleep recently when I realized with a start that I was still organizing a community project in my head. I then took several deep breaths to help me refocus and said, "Thank you, God, that I have a roof over my head, a comfortable bed, and perfect pillow." I shifted my consciousness to my body and became aware of the coolness of the sheet, the warmth of my comforter. I don't remember anything after that…

God is "speaking" to all of us 24/7, if we have "ears to hear"; if we're "listening." God speaks through storms, bugs, rocks, baby feet, movies, turtles, meter readers, silence, wars, wrinkles – all the "stuff" of life. Allowing the message to come through is a choice, a conscious decision that can be cultivated and become second nature with practice.

If you don't have this kind of relationship and want to, begin by practicing appreciation for those around you.

I was in a meeting recently with a person whose personality resembled a steamroller. When I offered my input, their eyes flashed and their lips became a thin line; clearly, it was preferred that I be seen and not heard. I told a friend later that I recognized myself in this person, and if that was how I appeared to others when I was in "drill instructor mode", I had some changes to make.

To me, this was God speaking, helping me see where I could become more considerate and encouraging of others. Also, to lighten up; few things are so important that The Golden Rule can't be maintained.

Take the time to be "present" with the One that loves you more than any other.

May 4, 2002

God's always sending signals, whether we tune in or not

Did you ever notice how you see a plethora of Huggies and Nice 'N Easy hair color commercials during daytime TV, and Pepcid and Verizon ones after dinner? And later in the evening come the Mitsubishi ones (I love those!) and Victoria's Secret? These ads aren't just thrown in to a day's programming willy nilly. They're plugged in to what advertisers hope are the most receptive audiences.

I'm a morning person, not a night person. I can force myself to work in the evening, but by 9 p.m., after getting up at 4 a.m., my synapses aren't firing in the proper sequence. I can do stuff that doesn't require mental acuity, like folding laundry, but I can't study and retain anything. I am most receptive, perceptive, sharp and rarin' to go at 6 a.m.

My TV isn't hooked up to cable, so I'm always shifting the rabbit ears this way and that to bring in a station. Both ears straight up for Channel 9, left up, right to the 3 o'clock position for Channel 5. Point them towards the strongest wave of invisible beam and there you are. But if you're trying to get Channel 9 in where you get 5, clear reception is nonexistent.

Where are your rabbit ears pointing? Or are you on cable? With cable you can get just about any channel at any time with perfect clarity.

When are you most receptive to God? If you perceive God as only being available in a specific building during specific hours, you're missing a lot. Being "receptive to God" includes, but isn't limited to (a little legal lingo) finding God's love in a pink slip, a flat tire in January, an unfavorable diagnosis. If you can cultivate being receptive to God in and under all circumstances, you're a step closer to "praying without ceasing." Because prayer isn't always a formula learned in that building – its like they say about losing weight: avoid the diet (a temporary fix) and go for a lifestyle change. When you recognize that there is never a time when you are separated from God's love (we're the ones who close the circuit for whatever reason), you blossom like a flower that never wilts.

Can you see God in your walls? The ink cartridge for your inkjet?

"Say what?"

Well, where do the materials come from? God creates not only the animated human, but also what the human becomes after the breath of God departs it.

I believe God is present in all creation. And it doesn't depend on what direction your rabbit ears are pointed. Turn in any direction, and then look in a mirror.

Who couldn't appreciate going through life with a best friend who loves you no matter what? Who is there for you to depend on and draw strength from, no matter what?

Choose to be receptive to God who loves you just as you are. Always.

May 18, 2002

"Live Life On Earth As Though It's Heaven"

What do you think heaven will be like? Take a minute or two now and answer that question, please.

Maybe you came up with something like, "It will be peaceful, no fighting", or "I'll be with Jesus." OK, that's fine. But try to go deeper. Do you have any real sense of what heaven is going to be like?

Most folks I've talked with over the years envision heaven as a place of idyllic peace and beauty; where the lion has laid down with the lamb. In other words, where opposing forces have reconciled. Where there is no conflict or injustice; all souls are free of pain and guilt. A place where we all just "get along."

In the "Our Father" we read, "Thy kingdom come, thy will be done, on earth as it is in heaven."

We are acknowledging that God's will is done in heaven, and we are praying that it be accomplished on earth as well. Earth is the planet of polarities. It's an uphill struggle.

Think of a child growing up. At first, it has no idea it is separate from its mother. Around two years of age, the child discovers that it is an individual and begins to assert its desires and wants. The rest of the person's journey on earth is spent experiencing light and dark, good and bad, pain and joy. And yet, on some level, we ache for home. Our real home, back in what we call "heaven."

If we were to actually take that prayer to heart, and cooperate with its intent, how could we bring heaven to earth? It seems like we pray for peace but often sabotage our goal. We do our best to separate ourselves into little boxes that define us, i.e. I'm a Swedish (box) conservative (box) Protestant (box) in the USA (box) that believes (lots of boxes here.) Many of these boxes, these "separators" are benign; others, however, drive nails into our spirits. When I think of all the names I've been called in my life (I'm a large Polish female that wears glasses-you get the picture), I am reminded how much damage "boxes" can do.

It seems like our whole "tour of duty" here is defined by opposites and choices, issues and beliefs. There is no need of that in heaven; we're all one with the One.

If it is your goal to assist in making that prayer real, there are some concrete things you can do to facilitate it:

- Pull the reins in a bit on getting your own way; you don't always have to be right. If it isn't a matter of safety or ethics, does your will have to squash someone else's?
- This is a world of "choice." Think about whether your choice of words or behavior brings peace or division, harmony or discord. We do so much to defend our rights, our "lifestyle"; the price can be too high.

What can you do today to bring earth and heaven closer together?

June 1, 2002

It's what you're worth to God that matters

Many moons ago, I had a boyfriend who loved me and I him. I remember walking very early one summer morning, thinking about how that made me feel. Words like "invincible", "powerful" and "beautiful" filled my mind, and I felt very strong. It translated over to my everyday life. Standing alone, it was just "me." But his belief in me, and his decision to love me (as I thought about it much later), seemed to make me into a different person. I felt very clear-headed and purposeful in whatever I was doing. The speed bumps of life smoothed themselves out before me. It was like nothing I've experienced before or since, in a human relationship.

When we broke up, I lay on the floor and cried. Was it all a lie? As easily as his words inflated the balloon of my heart, his departure was the pinprick that sent me spiraling around the room, falling flat on my face.

Being the introspective soul that I am, I have gleaned a lot of wisdom from this event, and even though it was terribly painful for me, I wouldn't change a moment of it.

Whenever we give another human being the ability to define our self-worth for us, we limit our ability to grow into the fullness our Creator intended for us.

Take a close look at your life. From the time you were an impressionable child, you were a sponge soaking up everything you saw and heard about yourself and others. And not just from your family. Television, school, church, sports – everything you're exposed to in this world has a "position." What's "in" today could be "out" tomorrow. Remember Twiggy, hula-hoops, and candy cigarettes?

What I have come to understand, and am integrating all the time, is that there is only one true, unbiased source that can speak with unquestionable authority on my - and your - worth and value as a person, and that is our Creator.

The Creator I believe in doesn't make you run an obstacle course to be worthy of "unconditional love." There isn't anything you can do or say in order to earn your way into this affection. As human beings, we may set up "qualifiers" and find ways to exclude others, but that's because we're human, living in a polarized world.

God is so much more than that! God sees you – you! – as a precious soul, created in It's image. What you look like, who you vote for, what church you attend (or not), matters not to God, in my opinion. It's what you "really" are that God sees. It's that part of us that lives in eternity. It's what we revert back to when our body dies.

What we are tasked to do in this lifetime, it seems to me, is to find our way back to our beginning. Because once we know what we really are, and live it out, and pass it on, our "spark of divinity" will be fully aglow and we'll have heaven on earth.

June 15, 2002

Father's Day brings mixed emotions

Tomorrow is Father's Day. I don't usually address the event since my dad passed on just after my fifth birthday. And my stepfather, who came into the picture when I was nine, was an abusive alcoholic who threw my pregnant mother down a flight of stairs; she miscarried. It wasn't until I was older and saw how much my brother Chet, and my then brother-in-law Don, loved their families that I had a clue what a "good dad" looked like.

My son's father, shortly after we divorced, left town. Having full access to his son didn't keep him nearby. He wanted to live where it was warmer, he said. We are both grateful that contact has been made recently, and they are patching things up. For that, we both thank God.

God is referred to by Jesus as his Father. I can't think of a mainstream religion that doesn't see God as male. Considering the times these religions were formed, it makes sense. If Jesus had referred to the Creator as mother, a female without power in most parts of the world at that time (at present as well), he would not have been listened to, I don't think. Look at how we've distorted who Jesus was, too. We've been taught to have this mental picture of him as a tall, slender, white European, yet he was a dark-skinned, Middle-Eastern Jewish male.

Most of us believe that all souls are created in the image of their Creator. God is not male. Or female. God is genderless yet contains both within Itself (I used this word in a previous column and it was edited out, yet I feel it is most accurate.)

I know growing up I wondered where I was, as a female, in the Trinity of Father, Son, and Holy Spirit. Some advocate that the Holy Spirit is the "feminine face of God", but I can't think of a single instance where, as a child or even an adult, a pastor presented this understanding as a means to show females that they are a part of their Creator like males are.

So I grew up wanting to know how I fit into the picture. Am I not a part of God? Were females created as inferior - not good enough to be included as a part of God? How could a loving Father treat his daughters this way?

As I got older and did more research, asked more questions and listened more, I came to an understanding of God that allows me to "see myself" in my Creator. I'm a soul on a journey, just as you are. We're spiritual beings having a human experience.

So tomorrow, when you're thinking about your dad, see him with different "eyes." If you were fortunate, he loved you and cared for you in a way that helped you reach your highest potential. If he didn't, forgive him and pray that he – and you – find yourselves in God. It will give you strength and courage to continue on.

June 29, 2002

Make today count with God

I am not a neatnik by nature. Dishes can sit in the sink for a couple days; vacuuming is not a high priority. In other words, I am not tidy. I can be motivated to do so, however.

There was a problem with my dishwasher a couple weeks ago. Calling maintenance would mean someone would have to enter my abode. There is only me in my apartment. You'd think I could keep it neater than it is. I guess it's not a high enough priority. I'd rather be reading or writing or working on some project. After chastising myself soundly, I set to cleaning up the joint. It only took an hour.

"What's the big deal?" I always ask myself when I find myself in this predicament. "Why do I keep putting it off?" The loud voice in my head said, "It's because you're lazy! Duh!" I think its just because I don't like housework. If I had more money I'd hire someone to do it for me.

There are scads of people who don't call on God until they need help in some way, or are otherwise "motivated" to reach out to the "Repairman", if you will.

Contacting God could go something like this.

"Dear God. Hi, my name is (fill in the blank) and I've got a problem. We just found out our son is doing drugs and we need your help."

What does this make God? And what does it say about your relationship with your Creator? Alan Cohen states, "The spiritual path is not one of attainment, but return." Spiritual writer Pierre Teilhard de Chardin wrote, "We are not human beings having a spiritual experience; we are spiritual beings having a human experience." And St. Teresa of Avila said, "The life of the spirit is not our life, but the life of God within us." An unattributed quote I love is, "God is not in me like a button is in a glass of water. God is in me like the ocean is in a wave."

God is within us. Sometimes we live it in a small way, sometimes in a big way. St. Theresa writes, "Our Lord does not care so much for the importance of our works, as for the love with which they are done."

We are first and foremost souls on a mission, I believe. We are "chips off the Old Block", manifestations of our Creator, capable of tremendous acts of compassion and kindness, forgiveness and awe. We are co-creators with the Creator of all that is seen and unseen. So often we let our human vision incapacitate us and blind us to what we truly are. Fear veils our internal eyes and heart, keeping us from stepping out, taking a risk and being true to our calling.

For you have been called. Called into being by God, to help create heaven on earth, to be an instrument of peace and healing. What are you doing today to make it so?

July 27, 2002

Forgiveness Day: a time to start over

If you were to stop right now and think on what is causing you the most personal pain, it would most likely be related to a relationship.

Perhaps it's a family member who forgot your birthday, someone who took your friends life, or a boss that doesn't listen to you.

Why do these things weigh so heavy on our hearts? One thing they all have in common is a sense of loss, and perhaps betrayal.

I was angry with my Dad for years as a teen. He was a "brittle diabetic" who ate candy bars. This was back in the late 50's when they used glass syringes that had to be boiled to be cleaned. Didn't he love me enough to want to stay alive? Why didn't he stay away from something he knew was bad for him? This haunted me for years until I was able to reconcile it. I realized I needed to forgive him in order to be free of the at-times overwhelming pain. It was draining the joy from the rest of my life. Once I forgave him, my life changed. It was as if the first domino had been toppled, and the "door to my perception" was altered. I saw so many things differently.

Who do you need to forgive, understanding that it benefits you more than the recipient?

Forgiving someone doesn't mean they're off the hook for their behavior. It doesn't mean that you cease to feel the loss. Most often it's a process that takes time and the willingness to relinquish the pain and anguish. It's possible to become comfortable with those emotions, and feel a loss when you give them up. But there is something better. There is healing available.

On Sunday, August 4th, Kitsap County will observe its first International Forgiveness Day, an ecumenical event focused on bringing attention to the healing power of forgiveness. On June 10th, our county commissioners signed a proclamation stating that the first Sunday in August, hereinafter, would be named so. Forgiveness is good for everyone.

At Marina Park in downtown Port Orchard, from 1 p.m. to 3 p.m., a host of local folks will speak. They include Commissioner Jan Angel, Rev. Chet McVay, Ross Murker, Gabe Santana, Carmel Pennington and myself. The event is free.

For most religions/denominations, forgiveness involves God forgiving us, us forgiving each other, and forgiving ourselves. For many, their heartfelt connection with their Creator is strained or broken because they're angry with God for not providing a physical healing, or "allowing" some horrific loss to occur. This will be addressed as well.

Rabbi David Wolpe writes, "The human heart carries hurts through life. We are all scarred, burdened and broken in different ways. Many of these injuries are unavoidable. We cannot escape the losses that life brings. But we control whether our souls are tied in knots, angry and gnarled. We cannot control the world, but we are each of us the captains of our own souls."

You have it in you to forgive.

August 10, 2002

Trying to see good in harm done to you

A reader of this column turned me on to the writing of retired Baptist pastor, the Rev. Rodney Romney. Most recently, he was with Seattle First Baptist Church. He continues to teach, preach and otherwise enjoy his retirement. A web search revealed a lot about his theology and life. I can hardly wait to meet him.

She forwarded one of his sermons, which I enjoyed immensely. I subsequently checked a book of his out of the library. It's titled "Wilderness Spirituality" and it's not about loving nature (although that is a part of it.) It's about the journey of faith we all travel, and it's outstanding. I'm going to buy it so I can highlight, underline, etc. and not worry about who gets it next.

The sermon dealt with Joseph (of the Bible) whose brothers sold him into slavery, only to meet him years later when they faced a famine. Joseph, now second in command behind Pharaoh, was in charge of the grain reserves. It spoke about their fear of his reaction, now that he was in a position to do them harm. Would he deny them assistance? Would he need retribution?

They stand in his presence, and Joseph says something that to this day holds wisdom for us. He says (paraphrased), regarding their sale of him as a child, "You meant to do harm, but God meant it for good."

When I first read that sentence, it bounced around inside my thoughts like a bearing in a pin-ball machine. I was thinking of all the occasions, both personal and planetary, that this applied to. And it immediately connected with a favorite Scripture: "All things work together for good for those that love God." (Rom. 8:28)

It can be impossible at first to see how God can bring good from what you consider devastation, but if you turn your mind towards finding it, it will eventually reveal itself.

Our families and our nation cried and agonized most recently over the events of 9-11 (and we continue to be horrified and saddened by the bombings and loss of life throughout the world.) Yet with some distance now we can see how it has galvanized people into a greater appreciation and love for who and what we have in our lives.

In our daily living we all face situations where we or someone we love is being mistreated, or where we've experienced harm at the hands of another. The urge to return to them what they have given us can be overwhelming. Yet look at Joseph's response.

"You meant to do harm, but God meant it for good."

What powerful words of hope! If God is for you, who can be against you? You aren't going to see this in your life, however, unless your face is turned toward God. Unless it is your desire to "love God with your whole heart, soul, mind and strength" it can be almost impossible to understand that you can get "beauty for ashes."

Turn your heart toward God and find peace.

August 24, 2002

"Forgive God, Cherish The Gift Of Free Will"

At our first "International Forgiveness Day in Kitsap County" event earlier this month, Carmel Pennington spoke on a potentially touchy subject: forgiving God. I thought it took great courage on her part to speak what a lot of folks feel but are afraid to come right out and say – that they're mad at God.

Rev. Rodney Romney addresses this in his book, "Wilderness Spirituality." He writes, "Most of us think it's audacious and sinful to imagine that we would ever need to forgive God for anything. Yet buried deep inside is often a sense of anger against God for not doing something about the bad things that are in this world and over which we seem to have little control."

Every single day someone cries out, "Why did God allow this to happen? Why didn't He send his angels to warn him/her/them/us?" There is anger, frustration and disappointment because we forget that God allows the sun to shine – and the rain to fall – on all souls. We forget that we were created with free will.

I attended a funeral recently at First Lutheran Church in Port Orchard. Pastor Allen Cudahy was conducting the service for his mother-in-law, Nancy McCracken, who was killed in a motorcycle accident the previous week. Her other son-in-law, Jake Jefferson, sang at the beginning of the service. I was awestruck by the strength and love these two showed for her, and for us, by being there in those capacities.

Allen's sermon revealed his anguish and the family's immense sense of loss. He spoke of Nancy's commitment to God, family and community. I was very deeply touched by his efforts to forgive the person who caused the accident that took her life and left her husband in critical condition. He said, as I recall, "Who among us has not slid through a red light, passed when we shouldn't have, tail-gated, or otherwise failed to obey the law? The accident was not God's fault; it had nothing to do with His love for her. An individual made a bad choice that took a life."

Rev. Romney states, "There are certain things that God can do and will do. But there are also things that God cannot do or will not do. God will not abrogate that precious and often painful gift of human freedom given to us on our day of creation, no matter how unwisely or harmfully we choose to exercise it. In other words, God is limited by the God-imposed laws of this universe."

He continues, "The one thing God does with all of us is to suffer with us when we suffer, and to forgive us continually, even when we are struggling with our anger against God. We do not see the whole picture of what God is doing, and we have only meager scraps of information as to what God really is."

It turns out Nancy's favorite Scripture verse is mine, too. "Love God with your whole heart, soul, mind and strength. And your neighbor as yourself." Do this, and peace is yours.

September 7, 2002

"Join With Others To Heal National Wounds"

Next week marks the first anniversary of the Sept. 11 tragedy. I've spoken with folks who plan on avoiding any televised programs related to it, or participating in any gatherings to commemorate it. There are people, too, who state they'll be having candle light services and prayer vigils. We have different ways of dealing with pain and healing. Let's honor each other's journey with respect and compassion.

Recently my fall edition of "Spirituality and Health" magazine arrived. The issue is titled "Healing…while life goes on" and it contains many articles and reflections stemming from that traumatic day.

Editor Robert Owens Scott writes, "This is a special issue for us because it is all too close to home. As we look out from our offices at the ongoing work at Ground Zero, we can't help but be drawn back to that day. We can't help feeling grateful to be alive."

An article by Margaret Wheatley, titled "No One Is Saved By Silence", goes into the healing power of telling our stories. The healing that occurs when others just listen to us without judgment or needing to "fix" things.

"In Western culture," she states, "it is common to keep our pain to ourselves. The greater the suffering, the more we withdraw. We've been taught to bear trauma privately, to get on with life. And we who have not suffered trauma often silence the suffering ones. We don't want to hear their stories because we won't know what to say. When others voice their pain, grief, loss and despair, we believe we must fix it or make it go away, that it's not enough just to listen. The tragic irony is that silence creates more trauma."

That may well hold for personal trauma, but the nation has learned to grieve as a whole after the events of Oklahoma City, Columbine and September 11th, among others. We stared at our television screens in disbelief as the unimaginable happened. We cried together, hugged our loved ones longer together, and healed together as we gave voice to our individual experiences.

On Wednesday, at Bremerton High School's Memorial Stadium, there will be a community-wide observance titled "September 11: Kitsap United in Memory." Beginning at 7 p.m. there will be first-person remembrances, music, and moments of reflection. This is a good opportunity for you to join with others in binding our national wounds with collective prayer and heartfelt compassion.

I find it difficult, when thinking of those events, not to think of the people suffering from suicide bombings on the other side of the world. They have no sense of security. No optimism that the horror will end any time soon. They are confronted every day with the specter of destroyed buildings, missing loved ones and immeasurable loss. Such sorrow.

While our community's love and healing thoughts are focused on the heroes and survivors of September 11th next week, let us also remember our sisters and brothers throughout the world who identify with our loss; who understand devastation, fear and vulnerability. Let us pray that God's wisdom continue to guide us all in the days ahead.

September 21, 2002

"Finding The Rainbow After The Storm"

Last week was the first anniversary marking the September 11th tragedies. The papers and airwaves were saturated with analysis, specials and first person stories. There was so much detail.

I've only had cable for my TV a couple weeks and was channel surfing from the comfort of my couch one afternoon. I was clicking through the stations and ended up on some channel that was showing a documentary on the local people who had taken pictures of the devastation of the twin towers.

Pictures are so powerful. I didn't want to see anymore; I was crying. But I couldn't seem to move away from witnessing their stories. Observing the pain and misery of others can have merit if it moves you to make changes that, even incrementally, foster peace and reconciliation.

What will you take away from that day, ultimately? What good can come from it that will specifically affect you, who are so far away from Ground Zero? We allow good to come from evil when we learn something from it that improves humanity, and I believe that happens when we ask our Creator for wisdom and guidance. You've heard so many family members of the victims say that their loved ones passing won't have been in vain if wakes you up to living life consciously. If you grow in appreciation of the love and wonder you have in your life now. If you cherish the sunrises, abilities and opportunities you have in your life right now. Focus on the phrase "...won't have been in vain..." We're always trying to find the rainbow after the storm because it gives us hope. We want to have made a difference in the world. We want our lifetime to count for something.

I saw a picture the other day of all the babies born to women whose mates had passed away due to the terrorist attacks. There must have been at least thirty newborns. They will have a unique bond with each other, and with us, as they grow up and into history. What kind of world will we give them to live in?

On the back cover of local author June Cotner's book, "Baby Blessings" is a verse written by Theresa Mary Grass titled "Our Wish for You". It reads, "May you always see beauty in the world and hear music every day. May you know the touch of gentle hands and walk the peaceful way. May the words you speak be loving, may laughter see you through. May you be blessed with hope and joy – these gifts we wish for you." This is what we hope for, for those children and the world's children.

How can we live a life that isn't in vain? We must all do what we can to promote peace on our planet and ensure that all our children are safe, healthy and happy. We must work together toward the greater good in all areas of our lives. And we need to appreciate and care for our blessed and beautiful earth.

October 5, 2002

"In Dark Times, Pray For Your Neighbors – All Of Them"

It's chilly this evening, and the rain can't be far behind. It's pretty dark around 7 – a.m. or p.m. Leaves crunch underfoot. And there's this scent in the air that is unmistakable – we're moving into fall.

Most years, fall and winter are fairly interchangeable. Maybe more gray in February. Overall, these days tend to be damp and dark. Fortunately, I love this weather! It's amazing to me how happy I am this time of year. Which is good because we aren't known for long stretches of sunlight. My favorite time is the transition from winter to spring. Some changes are easier to handle than others are - even welcome.

You know the old saying, "The only sure things in life are death and taxes." We need to add "change" to that list.

Recently my son's hours were significantly cut at his job site, forcing him to move. His car stopped running at the same time and he had no funds to fix it for weeks. His best friend was injured in a rollover traffic accident and he dropped off his dad's radar screen – again. Watching him react and adapt to all these challenges broke my heart and made me even prouder of him. In our discussions we acknowledged that when you have one or two painful changes in quick succession, you can hold it together with your family and friends for support. But when you get hit over, and over, with little or no time for emotional recovery between "hits", your ability to "bounce back from the punches" suffers. I describe this kind of life as "living on impulse power", or just getting by, instead of being in the preferred "warp drive."

How do you feel when you're in a lot of "negative" stress? Are you anxious - maybe fearful? Do you snap at others more easily and find that your decisions aren't always well thought through? Now, add to your personal stress the stuff happening in the world. While you may have some immediate control over what you can do for yourself and your family, you as an individual have very little control over what happens elsewhere that can effect your life greatly. Even the most even-keeled people I know now say they're concerned about our nation going into another war.

What is a soul to do with all this negativity going on in their life and that of friends and family? Pray. And for me, its not so much the "God, please give me the outcome I think is best" type, but the "God, may your will be done on earth as it is in heaven" type. Our "enemies" have families and economies, too. And we know so very little in reality about the "big picture."

So pray. Pray as if your life depended on it. Pray for wisdom and right thinking. Pray for your self, family, community and neighbor. Because our neighbor these days lives on the other side of the world as well as next door.

October 19, 2002

"Meth Affects Spiritual Community, Too"

Regular readers of The Sun will recall the excellent series of articles that are running this year on the methamphetamine epidemic in Kitsap County, titled "The Meth Toll." Julie McCormick has done a superior job, in my view, of capturing both the facts and feelings involved with this widespread problem. If you missed any of the articles, go to www.thesunlink.com and click on the title of the series.

I've been on our county's Drug Interdiction Task Force since it began (work related), and at one point I went around last year asking community leaders how they felt our meth situation was impacting their lives, work, etc. To a person they said, "What's meth?" then "What epidemic?" I'm hoping that the education The Sun is providing will help us all see what is happening to us; what is running through our communities like a virus, infecting and disrupting the lives of so many people.

The first few months on the task force, we were educated into the situation. Speakers from Child Protective Services, the Health Department, environmental protection and mental health groups, schools, coroner's office, WEST Net and other law enforcement, Naval Investigative Service, Harrison Hospital's emergency room physicians, apartment owners, etc., and former users themselves, brought us the facts. I can remember sitting at a table in Givens Center during one of our meetings, feeling stunned - like they were all talking about some other world. How could all this be going on around me and I didn't see it? That's when I started asking others about their perceptions and realized...it's just under the surface, like a subterranean tunnel.

This summer, while the task force was on its break, I began asking myself, "What is the spiritual community's response to this problem?" Granted, you probably will not find a meth user in a pew, but the officer who arrested them may be. The professional who is dealing with their children may be. Their mothers and fathers, teachers, retail managers and homeowners who have had goods stolen to support the addiction may be. So many children are negatively impacted by this, and may be with the grandparents in the fourth row.

And how do we minister to those making, selling, and using it? As totally abhorrent as their behavior is, they're still "one of us", still part of the human race. They are our sons and daughters and employees. They drive on our roads posing a risk to every one of us. It is of everyone's concern.

So I ask pastors and others everywhere: What is your response to this? How can you reach out to those in your churches and community that are suffering, perhaps silently, and in embarrassment? What else can be done? Please write to me and let me know how you address this issue, because we must face it head-on. I'm hoping to share with others the actions you take.

People of faith cannot go uncounted in this conflict.

November 2, 2002

D.C. area sniper shootings illustrate importance of not taking life for granted

It's over. Kids are back playing on the schoolyards in Maryland. People are filling their vehicles with gas, and going about the business of living.

Since there have been no further sniper shootings, and the weapon used has been recovered, folks feel confident that they got the assailants.

One thing I've heard repeatedly is that it could have been us. Can you imagine being afraid to leave your house for fear you'll be picked off like a tin can on a fence? Knowing there's a chance – a good chance you could step out your front door and not return home? Imagine the physical and emotional fall-out from such fear. Most of us can't control the flood of chemicals our bodies produce under these circumstances. Keep each other in prayer, please.

Our sensitivities are also heightened with all the discord going on in the world around us.

Undoubtedly, living in the Information Age has increased our stress a hundred fold. Knowing what occurs within a heartbeat of when it happens, anywhere on planet Earth, is available with the click of a mouse or remote control. Whether events occur in Israel, Russia, North Korea, Ireland or any other part of the globe, we hear about it instantly, in minute detail. Every day we see that our concerns are our neighbors as well.

I was thrilled to see the article on child safety in the Sun last Sunday. The Kitsap County Sheriff's Office, always sensitive, I believe, to the needs of the community, provided the paper with tips on how to protect our kids. In talking with mom's who are always looking for ways to increase their children's margin of security (and their peace of mind), they said this was information they could use immediately. We always seem to feel and function better when we believe we have some control over our lives, and that is what they gave us. The possibility of violence still exists, of course, but we have another tool in our arsenal of protection now.

We are to take reasonable precautions to protect our life and the lives of those we care about. There comes a time, however, when we've done all we can and face our mortality head-on. Sometimes you have time to reflect and make changes in your life that reveal your core priorities, sometimes you do not.

It's the rare person who knows the day they will pass over, leave this flesh and blood existence and return to the spiritual one they came from. We have been given a tremendous gift, and that is the awareness of a second chance. Are you taking circumstances and people in your life for granted, or are you "present?" If it means something to you to be all God intended you to be, are you putting off saying or doing what is in your heart? There may be no tomorrow; what do you want your life to say today?

November 16, 2002

Belief in God is a matter of faith and choice

"Dad, is there really a God?"

"What brings that up?"

"Reading about that Boy Scout in the paper. The one that was kicked out for not saying he believed there was one. Is there one?"

"What do you think?"

"Well, I know what you and Mom taught me. I believe there is one because you say so. How else would I know?"

Dad looks at his child's face. "How old are you now?"

"Twelve. I'll be thirteen in February. Why?"

"Because I was your age, maybe a little older, when my parents began teaching me how to find out about God for myself. Since you're asking the question, I'm thinking you're ready."

"You mean about prayer, Dad? I know all about that. I ask God for help everyday in school, and thank God for you and Mom, my bike, PlayStation 2 – stuff like that."

Dad smiled. "Praying is very good way to stay connected to God. I'm glad to hear you do it often. Prayers are a lot like air – invisible but you know it's working. Let me ask you this – how often do you think about God?"

"What do you mean?"

"Well, for example, how often do you look up at the stars and planets and think about where they all came from? Or think about what your soccer ball is made of?"

"I don't."

"If you take a little bit of time every day, like after you just wake up, and ask God questions like that, you'll start to build your own bridge."

"But Dad, that still doesn't answer my question. How do you know God is real? That there really is a God?"

Dad was lost in thought for a few moments then said, "There are people who will tell you God exists, and those that will tell you God doesn't. They will have proof that backs up their belief, and you'll wonder which one is right. What it comes down to is a matter of faith, and choice. I choose to believe there is a God because I can't conceive of you and planets and elephants and volcano's coming into existence on there own. I was taught that God was the creator of all that is seen and unseen, and I choose to believe it's true. I've prayed and thought about what I was taught growing up – some things I kept, others I didn't. If you ask God for guidance, and you're open to hearing it come from our church, music, friends, prayer, books and the like, I believe you'll get what you need. Over my lifetime, I've also had personal experiences that have confirmed God's existence for me. Again – someone else may say I deluded myself. Yet my spirit, my soul, tells me this is real. I have a relationship with God now. There will come a time when you know one way or the other. I can only tell you what I believe until then."

The child paused, nodded and said, "OK Dad. I understand."

November 30, 2002

Help your neighbors this holiday

There were three articles in The Sun I read this week that had to do with our economy. Two focused on food banks, the other on the hopes for strong holiday sales to bolster it. It's a sad commentary that our strength as a nation depends in part on how much we spend on Christmas.

The first article was from AP and it quoted Denise Agee, coordinator for St. Vincent de Paul in Bremerton.

"I can tell you that most of our clients that come into our food banks are employed," she said. "We're seeing more and more working individuals coming in now." She mentions that Navy families need to use the food banks, too. "That's pretty scary."

Then, in Wednesday's paper, we read another article on how food banks are struggling, what with all the job layoffs Washington is experiencing, and one on how the strength of the national economy is resting on strong "holiday sales."

Do you hustle by the bell ringer at the exit of a building? Even if it's only the coins in your pocket, every time you leave a store contribute to the pot. Change adds up; every dollar can go towards keeping the heat on in a house, purchasing a case of peas, or getting a pair of shoes for a second-grader. It's the very least you can do. The very least.

I spoke with Jennifer Hardison, executive director of South Kitsap Helpline in Port Orchard. They'll be caring for over 700 families this Christmas, farming out some to local churches and St. Vincent de Paul of Port Orchard. Businesses can adopt families through them, too. We've done that where I work at Peninsula Work Release.

Jennifer says they're seeing "a lot of new faces", and also an increase in the working poor. Contact them, or the "helping agencies" in your area, to see how you can contribute what is needed most.

For those of you who feel that those in need are not your responsibility, that you're not your "brother's keeper", let me point out a few things that may help you have a change of heart.

It is in your best interest to ensure no child goes hungry (any time of year) because undernourished kids with growling bellies have a difficult time concentrating and doing school work (no matter what grade they're in.) These are the folks who are going to be faced as adults with the reality we are creating today. They will be taking the responsibility for seeing to our care, as seniors. We want them to have healthy bodies, minds and spirits.

It is in your best interest to ensure that no adult/senior goes hungry because poor eating often results in a lowered immune system which translates into poor health and the concomitant costs.

If finding a benefit to yourself is the only way that you can see your way to helping others, so be it. But do it. Please. It'll be good for your soul.

December 14, 2002

We all come from the one source,
despite our differences

What do Santa, Homeland Security, and God, all have in common? They know whether you've been naughty or nice.

I had a cow when my favorite grocery chain started up those "we like you more than them" customer cards recently. And was relieved to know I could get the "savings" without losing any more of my identity to some databank that would track my purchases; they'll issue you a card without you putting one speck of ink anywhere. I don't mind somebody knowing how many eggplants are purchased. It does bother me for "them" to know, though, how many I bought. It just doesn't matter. Does it?

Most of us lose the understanding of our original "identity" as we grow and are socialized into our families and communities.

You'll remember the story about the parents who bring home the new baby and the little brother begs to be alone with her. The parents want their firstborn to accept the newborn, but are concerned over his pleading to be by himself when he speaks to her. They decide to turn up the volume on the nursery monitor and listen closely.

Lying in her crib, the baby gurgles and smiles. Her brother approaches her and says, "Please tell me about God. I've almost forgotten."

I totally believe in that message. As we grow, "mature", and learn the ways of the world, we lose the memory of our true self and our source. And this is true for all souls on this planet. Everyone is from the One Source and that is God, whatever we may call it.

Rev. Rod Romney, a retired Baptist minister living in Seattle, wrote an article recently titled, "What If God Is All There Is?" It states, "Jesus essentially taught that God is all there is. Nothing in life is apart from God, for all creation and all creatures carry God within. The birds of the air, the lilies of the field, all human creatures – all are loved by God because all are carriers of God."

All are loved by God.

All the signs are there. Around the world we are waiting for the "other shoe to drop." Troops are massing and "playing war games." Ships and personnel are being readied to engage in what would be a war unlike any other. With 21st century technology and training, we are poised to venture into combat.

I understand that I am not very well versed on politics; the plans and goals of our administration are not something I have full knowledge of. The religions of the world attribute different qualities to their "God." Still…still… we all bleed. We all love our children the best way we know how. We all want our way of life to survive. We all want to be safe from harm. We all want to live.

There are good people on both sides of this issue in this country. We can all, however, pray and work for peace and encourage dialogue.

No one wants to die.

December 28, 2002

Live in the present in 2003

In a few days, we'll usher in a new year. I enjoyed seeing the progress of this across the world as we rang in 2000; different customs, new sounds and ceremonies were revealed. Knowing how other cultures celebrated the event made the planet smaller for me. I knew my brothers and sisters better because of it.

As we take down our trees and ornaments from Christmas and rev up to bring in '03, a lot of folks take time to reflect back on how the present year went. Kind of a "lessons learned" flashback. We do this in hopes of not repeating past mistakes, and in anchoring "best practices." We also list wishes and resolutions for the future. Here are a few of mine.

A "best practice" was integrating the philosophy of "The Power of Now" by Eckhart Tolle. From it I have latched on to living in the present. You may think that we all do, but our pasts live on in the present, and are extended into the future. To a certain degree this is wise. For me, past losses and sorrows drove emotional responses and decisions. I had not moved on from them because I had not made the connection. Having done that now, a great burden was lifted from me. Hidden in the shadow, my history manipulated me. In the daylight, I could see how things tied together, and now make different choices. This will be an on-going process.

I've never paid much attention to New Year's Resolutions. I figure, if something is worth doing, start now. I do have a couple wishes, though, and they're for all of us.

1. I wish that we lived moment to moment with the understanding that there is no place where God is not, because God is not separate from creation. Just as God allows the rain to fall on "good and bad alike", all that is "seen and unseen" is of God. The earth, and all that is on it and in it; the oceans, with their vast uncharted depths; the expanding universe... all of God. There is no place where God is not, no situation where God cannot be found...if God is sought.

2. I wish we could see each person as a manifestation of his or her Creator. We would look at each other differently, treat each other differently. I see all of us, all souls, as a teaspoon of the ocean, God being the ocean. As individuals, we don't see what we came from. We see ourselves as separate little bits. We don't recognize what we are, what we can be if we come together. Most often we acknowledge with our heads, not our hearts, that a spark of divinity is within us, having been made in the image of God. That spark is our teaspoon of Ocean.

May we work together in '03 to create peace by listening more deeply, forgiving more completely, and wanting the best for each other.

2003

January 11, 2003

Read the Bible, along with these books

Here is my annual column on spiritual reading and resources. It provides food for reflection, which is the goal of this column.

My top four books this year are:

- "Wilderness Spirituality" by Rev. Rodney Romney. You can get it through the library or from Amazon.com. Regular readers know Rev. Rod is the retired senior pastor from Seattle First Baptist Church. This is his latest book and covers his own spiritual journey. It impacted me deeply and helped me understand a lot of my own experiences.
- "Prayer Notes to a Friend", by Fr. Ed Hayes. Available from his publisher's website, www.forestofpeace.com, or Amazon.com, this small volume is a collection of his reflections and wisdom to "friends." Fr. Ed has published a wealth of excellent reading, including last year's referral, "St. George and the Dragon."
- "The Power of Now", by Eckhart Tolle. It has taken me a couple years to fully understand and integrate the contents of this book. Hopefully you won't find it so difficult! It is, however, well worth the effort.
- "The Journey Inward – Quotations for the Soul" by Rosalie Maggio is available only from Barnes and Noble. I love this book! I spent a few minutes with it in friend Asha's house and went out and bought it immediately. It's great inspiration and reinforces my favorite quote, from Socrates, "The unexamined life isn't worth living."

Right now I am reading "A New Christianity for a New World" by Bishop John Shelby Spong. He is called a lot of things, one being "the most liberal cleric." When I started reading this book, I remembered how scared I was years ago when I contemplated attending a service in a church that wasn't my denomination. I had been raised to believe that the wrath of God would come down upon me if I considered attending a service elsewhere, or read anything that didn't have an imprimatur attached to it. It will definitely stretch your mind.

There are three websites that I routinely peruse that provide excellent spiritual book and movie reviews. They are www.spiritualityhealth.com, www.beliefnet.com, and www.gracecathedral.org.

I have two periodicals that cause me to literally squeal with joy when I find them in my mailbox. They are "Spirituality and Health" (see website above) and "Sacred Journey" (www.sacredjourney.org).

To feed my soul I also read Rev. Dale Turner's column (www.seattletimes.com), visit "Astronomy Picture of the Day (http://antwp.gsfc.nasa.gov/apod/astropix.html),

"The Daily Motivator" (www.greatday.com/motivate/index.html), "Theology Today" (http://theologytoday.ptsem.edu/main-frame.htm), "www.gratefulness.org", "www.spirituality.com", and a lot of sites that feature nature and quotes.

I have four quotes on the wall next to my computer. I see them frequently which reinforces their messages. They are, ""Take your mind off the problem and put it on God", by Norman Vincent Peale; "There are two ways of spreading light – to be the candle or the mirror that reflects it", by Edith Wharton; "Thank you for everything. I have no complaints whatsoever", author unknown to me; and last but not least, "Cowabunga!" by Snoopy.

Decide to make it a happy New Year!

January 25, 2003

Keep searching for war resolution

My brother, Chet, will be 60 this year. He served in Vietnam as a Marine sergeant all of '66. H & S Company, 3rd Battalion 5th Marines. I remember mom paying rapt attention to "The Huntley / Brinkley Report" on TV when there was news of the war. I couldn't believe my big brother was there, so far away. I was 10, he was 20. I didn't think I could love him or miss him any more than I did. When he came home I was 14, and he was a different person. That's to be expected when someone sees and does things they never dreamed of. No amount of training, he says, prepares you for the real horrors of war.

I heard a lot from him growing up about his experiences. Some stories were funny, like the one about all the "boots" on the USS ORISKANY and their adventures with seasickness. Others I couldn't comprehend. Like his stepping over blown off body parts while eating a ration of canned fruit cocktail. I don't know how he's made it all these years with memories like that.

All this has come up again for him because we are on the precipice of war. He's observing the ships deploy, the build up of troops; he's listening and watching the president. He called me the other night because, he said, he had to talk to somebody. I recount part of our conversation with his permission.

"Sal, I feel like it's a tidal wave that is going to wash over us. We say Saddam is dangerous, and he is. But to get to him, because he's a bully and a coward, we'll have to bomb Baghdad like we bombed Berlin. We're going to go in there and our young men and women are going to die, and their women and children and families are going to die. We'll end up killing several hundred thousand women and children. We cannot do this on our own. If the United Nations agrees its necessary, that's one thing. We should not do this unilaterally.

What bothers me most, Sal, is President Bush wants to go to war too much. Why? I don't want the blood of the innocent on my hands. This nation was founded on Christian principles. Seems that Bush wants revenge. Are we going to wish we had done more to resolve this after they start shipping the body bags home? I don't think we've exhausted every possibility for resolution on this yet.

There are times when we have to fight to defend a weaker neighbor or ourselves, but we aren't there yet. Sometimes you have to fight fire with fire. We have to be patient and let the inspectors do their job."

It's an immense responsibility, sending our sons and daughters, moms and dads into harms way. Please continue to pray and work for peace. We all have so much to lose. As the Rev. Martin Luther King, Jr. said, it's "Non-violence or non-existence."

February 8, 2003

Turning to faith in time of tragedy, war

Who among us was not shocked and heart-broken to hear of last Saturday's devastating Columbia disaster? As the week progressed, family members, NASA officials and former astronauts were seen, heard, and spoke of those lost aboard the shuttle. The bio of each explorer revealed a soul in love with creation; a person passionate about space, learning, and contributing to world knowledge. Just as our military, law enforcement, and fire suppression personnel daily lay their lives on the line for the health and safety of others, so do our astronauts, who venture to fly beyond the boundaries of earth.

A headline on beliefnet.com this week read, "Seven Heroes, Seven Faiths" and stated that each person belonged to a different faith tradition. They were Hindu, Roman Catholic, Jewish, Charismatic, Unitarian, Episcopalian and Baptist. Together they lived, worked, and respected each other's beliefs and services. Suspended as they were above Mother Earth, perhaps their perspective on priorities was a bit different from those of us landlocked. They found a way to accept each other and love each other as they were; a very ecumenical group.

It seems probable at this moment in time that the United States will be at war in the near future. Thinking of all the prayers that families, friends, and others will express on their behalf, I wondered about how the military was sustained spiritually. I spoke with Chaplain Swanson at Sub Base Bangor.

I told him that it might be helpful for those sending their family members into harms way to know they would have access to religious guidance and services.

"In a nutshell, military chaplains are there to guarantee that our service members and their families can freely exercise their religious freedom," stated Swanson.

There is usually a chaplain with each major unit or ship. Each represents their own faith, i.e. Lutheran, Jewish, Muslim, etc. If a service person finds that the clergy assigned to them isn't of their tradition and the differences in expression are significant (for example, Lutheran and Jewish), a lay leader can be trained and appointed before deployment to fill the need. The chaplain will also work to hook them up with someone of their faith group, for support.

Chaplains, although non-combatants, can be found near the front lines with troops, and always at "casualty collection points" where they are available for prayer, guidance, and last rites. They see themselves as a very ecumenical team, working to meet the spiritual and religious needs of their military family. We owe them a huge debt of gratitude for the solace, wisdom, and hope they convey.

For more information on military chaplains go to www.chaplain.navy.mil or www.usachcs.army.mil. And check out spiritualityhealth.com's latest e-course, "Spiritual Literacy in Wartime."

Our nation has been wounded deeply in the last couple years. It seems like we barely recover one disaster before we're faced with another.

Mother Teresa said, "If we have no peace, it is because we have forgotten that we belong to each other." The world is very small, and we must all work for peace.

February 22, 2003

Ways to keep anxiety, fears at bay

Visiting with friend Asha over coffee recently, the discussion turned toward the tense world situation. Living in a military environment with all the installations nearby can leave you feeling like a sitting duck, we agreed. Hearing North Korea could reach the West Coast with its nuclear bombs did nothing to ease our growing sense of impending disaster.

Informing me that her husband, who works at a local Navy base, was being loaned to one out of state for a few months, her eyes filled with tears and her firm voice trembled. "At least he'll be out of harms way if anything should happen," she said softly.

"I understand," I said, nodding my head. "Every time – every single time Gabe (my son) goes out the door, I'm conscious that I may never see him again." We reached across the table to touch hands and blink back our emotions.

In the past when we've gone to war, we've literally "gone to war." Now, in the wake of 9/11, we realize that it make take shape right here on our own shores, in our own neighborhoods. There are over a half dozen countries with nuclear capability, and not all of them like us.

How do people of faith deal with fear?

An acquaintance of mine in high school told me, "Everybody I talk to about this blows it off; they say nothing is going to happen. But look at people boarding up their homes and buying up water and food. They're getting gas masks and inoculations for smallpox. People are scared. I am, too."

In dealing with anxiety, this may help hold you together.

- Turn off the evening news now and then.
- Stay in the "now." At the present time, we are not at war with Iraq. Even if you think it's inevitable, it isn't here yet. Years ago when times were tough, I'd have to remind myself, "Today we have a roof over our heads. Today we have food on the table." Don't borrow trouble; stay in the present.
- Do what you reasonably can to ensure your safety. If you were preparing for an "act of God" such as a tornado, or heavy snow or rainstorms, you'd be prepared. Have a first aid kit, gallons of water, non-perishable food, a change of clothes and blankets, a set of your prescriptions and a battery-run radio in a safe place, ready to use.
- Norman Vincent Peale said the way through problems is to "take your mind off the problem and put it on God." Most often, I interpret this to mean, do something good for others. If you're working all day and can't get to a school to read to kids or help out at a food bank, serve on a community or church committee. Volunteer with Special Olympics. Coach your kid's Little League team. Help your brother with his homework.

And pray. Leave the door open for "how" it's accomplished, and just ask that God's will be done.

March 8, 2003

Learn to 'love' your enemies

The Bible is full of hard sayings, like "Be perfect as your heavenly Father is perfect." (Matthew 5:48) Are we being asked to do the impossible?

Many of them, like the 10 Commandments, can help us stay on the "straight and narrow." When we don't like them, or can't see how they apply, we may choose to disregard them, or forget them altogether. My mom used to say, "It's easy to love when it's easy. It's when it's difficult that it really counts."

There is a direction given in the Bible that is easy to do when you don't have to do it.

"You have heard that it was said, 'You shall love your neighbor and hate your enemy.' But I say to you, 'Love your enemies and pray for those that persecute you, so that you may be children of your Father in heaven; for he makes the sun rise on the evil and the good, and sends rain on the righteous and unrighteous." (Matthew 5:43-45)

Define "enemy." It could be your neighbor who vociferously disagrees with your position on Iraq, or the leadership of a country that won't back our plans. Perhaps it's the U.N. Or maybe it's Saddam Hussein and Kim Jong II.

"Love Saddam? Are you nuts?" you may say. "I can certainly pray that they take him out quickly but that's about it." Still, there's that admonition. How do you do that? How can you ever love someone who has committed such inhumane acts? And why would you want to?

There are many different kinds of love. The kind of love you have for your kids or bowling buddies is different from the love you have for your spouse. The kind of love God has for all of us, saint or sinner, righteous or unrighteous, is the kind of love required here. It's called agape, and it heals a multitude of wounds. This is the kind of love that refuses to be overwhelmed by vengeance, jealousy or hatred. It means that, even though someone may not have mercy or compassion on others, you have it in your soul for them.

So what does this mean? That we allow Saddam and those who mistreat others to get away with their intolerable behavior? Not at all. We should pursue justice and fairness always. What it means is that we recognize that we are all God's creation; that the sun rises and sets for all of us.

Hating anyone hurts you, more than it does them; we know it can cause a multitude of illnesses over time. We are called to love as Christ loves, as difficult as that may be. This is the love that Gandhi had, and the Dalai Lama has for those who have persecuted their people.

Right now, we are so full of anger and fear. There is so much tension all over Mother Earth. Our lives are so interdependent upon each other for our survival. Let us pray for our enemies, and for ourselves.

March 29, 2003

Think of the children suffering in Iraq

Channel surfing recently, I came across a local cable station broadcast of a church group discussing the impending (as I write this) war with Iraq.

At one point, the pastor asked the question, "What are your strongest feelings around this issue?"

Snuggled up on my couch in comfy sweats, Diet Vernors chilling on ice beside me, I was jarred by the question. I knew what I'd been feeling for weeks but I hadn't put a name to it.

Listening, watching and reading everything I could, both locally and nationally, I always came back to the issue I felt was never fully addressed: what about the children?

Yes, I know how bad Saddam is. His regime tortures those who dare to criticize it. Loss of life doesn't stand in his way if there is something he wants.

Yes, I know no one wants war; no one wants to die or take a life.

Still, we're planning to drop so many bombs, and fire so many missiles, there's no way everyone can get out of the way. We know Saddam is likely to hide among the innocent, and we know a major goal is to rid the world of him. To what lengths are we willing to go to get him?

Is the fact that so many children will die so repugnant that our administration can't talk frankly about it? Is it seen as a consequence of war; something regretful, but to be expected and accepted? Every time I've heard the question asked it's dodged, and we're told the Iraqi people will be grateful we liberated them. But how can dead children, mothers and fathers, enjoy liberation? I understand Iraqi's as a people will be better off without Saddam, and this is the price to be paid. I just mourn all those, theirs and ours, that won't come home to their loved ones.

When our ground troops are in the streets, what are they going to see? Does the military prepare its soldiers psychologically for the carnage they'll encounter? Many of our young men and women (our kids) in uniform have children themselves; what are we doing to help them before and after they go into battle and behold all these little ones in pieces?

And what about the children? I'm told fifty percent of the Iraqi population is 15 years of age and under. Tens of thousands of children may lose their lives in this altercation. If the reverberations reach outside of Iraq to neighboring countries as predicted, including ours, how many more souls will go back to God?

My strongest feelings have been palpable grief and sorrow, loss and sadness.

I remember driving to an eye doctor's appointment on 9/11 and having the overwhelming feeling that I needed to pull over and pray that all the souls of those whose bodies had just died go to the light, go to their Creator.

Whatever your position on this issue, everybody is somebody's child. Think of the children. Pray for the children.

April 12, 2003

Finding comfort in God during war

"When you walk through a storm hold your head up high. And don't be afraid of the dark…"

Memories can be blessings or curses. They can arise from the shadows at a time least expected, or never leave you.

I was putting together a grocery list when this song came floating back into my consciousness from the archive in my mind.

"At the end of the storm is a golden sky and the sweet silver song of a lark…"

This was the song my brother, Chet, used to sing when he was in high school. When he left to join the Marines, and when he was over in Vietnam, I would cry myself to sleep singing it.

The situation we find ourselves in now is bringing back a lot of memories for veterans and those that lived through those times. The worries, the fear that someone in uniform may step onto your porch with grave faces. What would Mom do if Chet were killed? What would I do if we never got to watch another Lon Chaney spooky movie together? He would always go, "Moooooaahhhh!" and I'd shriek and he'd chase me through the house. What if he never came home? That's what people are feeling now. Mothers and fathers, friends and coworkers watch TV, hoping to catch a glimpse of someone they love.

"Walk on through the wind, walk on through the rain, though your dreams be tossed and blown…"

In his article, "War – from the Couch", Johann Christoph Arnold writes, "For most of us, this suffering is not very real. Statistically, most of us do not have loved ones in the Middle East. We are physically safe, and as the war unfolds in front of us – on TV, the Internet, the radio, and the daily paper – we may be momentarily shocked by images of brutality. For hundreds of thousands who do have family or friends in the Gulf region, however, the suffering is real enough. As stories of injury, capture, imprisonment, and death seep home from the front lines, it will become unbearably, overwhelmingly real. And unlike those of us who can turn off the TV set when it all becomes too much, these people will have no choice in the matter. They will have to grapple with the suffering of their loves ones until they find a purpose or meaning in it."

"Walk on, walk on, with hope in your heart and you'll never walk alone…"

God is with every suffering soul. We believe that God created all of humanity, and so we pray for guidance, and look for ways to help those suffering from the loss of life, innocence, and hope.

Clarissa Pinkola Estes states, "We cannot fix the whole world at once. We can, however, mend the part of the world that is within our reach. Any small, calm thing that one soul can do to help another soul, to assist some portion of this poor, suffering world will help immensely. What is needed for dramatic change is an accumulation of small acts adding to each other."

"… You'll never walk alone."

April 6, 2003

Not every answer is black and white when relying on prayer

A lot has been said in the media about President Bush's belief and reliance on what he understands to be divine inspiration from God. I don't really have a problem with that. Most of us pray to God, asking for direction, guidance, deliverance. And most of us, I'm thinking, receive "something" for our trouble; something that leads us to believe we've been heard and answered.

I don't think the concern was so much over the fact that he thought he'd heard from God, as it was he said it publicly, and what it led him to do. When you or I say, "God said…" it's usually followed by something like "… not to take your brother's bike," or "…I'm to take that job in Baltimore." Definitely not world changing. The stakes, while significant, aren't life threatening. There is always the possibility that we're not so much on the "hot line" with God, as we're listening to our own wishes.

Don't get me wrong. I'm a firm believer in communication with the Creator. It's just that we're human, and subject to misinterpretation and a host of other foibles.

Discernment is needed whenever divine guidance is received.

Another area of contention is, what one person or group believes God tells them may go completely in the opposite direction of what God is "telling" others. In this case, God "told" the president to go to war and rid the world of Saddam and his regime, while telling others that this war wasn't a "just" war, or war in any form is against God's will. Who is right? Good people with good hearts can believe in totally opposite "truths."

This situation fits alongside the "God is on our side, not on their side" issue. Does God want anyone to perish? This isn't an easy answer for me. You look at what terror Hitler and Pol Pot brought to the earth, and saying war of any sort is wrong doesn't seem right - they had to be stopped. Yet the taking of anyone's life, especially an innocent's, isn't right either, in my mind.

Everybody is somebody's child. Yet a child can grow into a person who has no regard for the sanctity of life. Do you meet them where they are, or raise the bar? I find myself in turmoil as I try to address these issues. My gut says that to take anyone's life is wrong; the Ten Commandments taught me that. Pastors I've talked with say that if it's legally sanctioned, however, such as in capital punishment or involvement in a "just war", taking another's life is permissible. I don't understand how we can get past "Thou shalt not kill", though. It seems pretty plain to me.

Every day we struggle to understand and do what's right. It is not always cut and dried, black or white. Even after asking for and receiving "feedback" from prayer, people of faith can disagree vehemently on issues. So how do we bridge this chasm? How can we bring forgiveness and healing amongst ourselves? Let's pray on that.

May 10, 2003

Make time for conversations with your close friend, God

Sometimes the simplest things can make your day.

Fixing dinner one night, my ears tune in to this grating voice coming from the TV in the living room. I poked my head around the corner to see what was on.

There were two cows laying quietly on grass in an idyllic setting, while this hyper-voiced rooster quizzed them on their peaceful dispositions. Not getting a response, he struts off the screen. One cow then says, "Wow." The other cow, turning its face aside as if to snicker, says, "Yeah. Poultry." I tell you, I bust a gut laughing. There's nothing quite like happy California cows, we learn; they make the best cheese.

Kudo's to the ad agency that put these spots together. I like them all!

We are barraged by voices and images trying to get us to buy or believe something. We are submerged in a sensory overload that doesn't always end at the end of the day. I swear, I wake up in the morning with my "To Do" list raring to go, as if I'd been working on it all night.

And what about our kids? They can drive you batty till you give in and buy the cereal/toy the ads have been pushing Saturday mornings. Technology has been both a blessing and a curse.

With all the demands for your attention, how do you find the time to think things through and make informed and conscious, not off-the- cuff, decisions?

It would be interesting to see the data on how the advent of cell phones passed across the world. Where and when did it begin, and how long did it take to saturate the earth?

Again, we gained – but we also lost. We pack more into 24 hours than at any other time in our history. You can send files to someone in London while sitting in your bathroom or car, at your kid's Little League game, or church. And as these wonders of communication continue to expand our expectations of life, our selves and each other, they also challenge us to set boundaries and priorities; not live life by default.

A couple months ago I came across a quote. I have since found versions of it everywhere. It says, "Water what you want to grow." In other words, direct your attention, behavior and energy towards that which you want to develop. In my case, I've altered my thinking from fear of the onset of medical complications, to the excitement of creating good health. It has had a profound effect on me.

Make it a priority to find a way to carve out some quiet time and settle into the silence with your Creator on a routine basis. Chat with God as if you were conversing with your best friend – because you are. Listen as you're told how much you're loved by the sound of the wind, birds chirping, a child or spouse sleeping deeply. It's there if you're listening.

Make time for God. God is always there.

May 24, 2003

This sermon on love offers some compelling thoughts

Have you ever had the experience where a particular word seems to pop up everywhere all of a sudden? The first time you come across it, you're just aware it's not routine for you; it stands out. Then, you hear or read it repeatedly. "What's up with that?" you may ask yourself. It's what I asked myself.

For the last couple of months, the word "compel" or "compelling" stood out for me. I'm one of those folks who believe in synchronicity, so I'm looking for a reason why this word, of all words, has taken center stage. It has my attention. Now what?

I was forwarded from friend Sky a sermon dated May 18, 2003, by the Very Reverend Robert V. Taylor, Dean of Seattle's St. Mark's Episcopal Cathedral (you can find it at www.saintmarks.org). "This is it!" my thoughts said before I even read it, and I knew this sermon was what I was compelled to pay attention to.

The title is "The Religion of Love is Like no Other" and it's based on 1 John 3:14-24. I found it incredibly powerful, honest, clear and straightforward. In the limited amount of words I'm allowed here I can't go into the detail I'd like; I hope you read it for yourself.

Taylor says, "Rumi (the Sufi poet) wrote that 'the religion of Love is like no other.' The author of the letter to the Johannine community believes the same thing. Yet he also knows that in our communal life we are resistant to the love that defines Christ. We are much more prone to love that serves us or benefits us or suits us. We might feign horror at such a thought! There is a simple test implied in today's Epistle and it is this: How is the reckless giving of self that defines the love and life of Jesus played out in your life?"

He continues, "This is our greatest challenge…how to be a people who are intentional and reckless about 'Christ love.' Christ love is radically different from being nice, polite, passive-aggressive with each other, or in a permanent snit. It is always an invitation to go beyond myself, beyond you, beyond our own collective self. It always comes out of a deep personal journey of walking through Yeats' 'places of excrement' and discovering how deeply you are loved by God."

How reckless are you in giving love and forgiveness? Do you subconsciously count the cost? Would your generosity and kindness cause you to "look" weak, uninformed, or otherwise questionable to those around you? Look deep to see beyond, as Mother Teresa would say, the "distressing disguise" we wear. Everyone has "battle scars" from life. Some try to hide them internally and they may become visible as addictions, others shove them in your face. Yet each of us comes from the same source. God created all souls. May we each love and forgive as we would like to be loved and forgiven.

June 21, 2003

All creatures matter

Even if you don't consider yourself a "religious" person, there is no denying that all of humanity is interconnected. Oftentimes, it's the cumulative contribution of a group that carries the greatest impact.

Do you doubt this?

Let's say you feel pretty safe, living on a farm in the Midwest. Food is fresh, air is clean… or is it?

My eyes widened when I read a report on air circulation from the Argonne National Laboratory, a United States Department of Energy facility operated by the University of Chicago. Titled, "Aerosols may travel halfway around the world", it states, "Years ago, we thought these particles (from 0.1 to 1 micrometer) didn't travel very far. Now we are realizing that they have lives of 20 to 60 days, which means they can travel halfway around the Northern Hemisphere. To take just one example, researchers are seeing air pollution from China carried by prevailing winds all the way to Seattle." It goes on to say that, "Even if you live on an Illinois farm, the air you breathe could carry pollution from Los Angeles."

Real time satellite downlinks connect the yoga master in India with students in New York, and the International Forgiveness Day event (forgivenessday.org) with the world.

What is the point of all this? The point is that you count. You, the retiree in Naples, FL, and you, the pastor in Mulvane, KS. The daily decisions you make can impact a child across town or across the world.

How you dispose of your garbage, the coffee and clothes you buy, the prescriptions you have filled – everything you do – effects someone, somewhere.

We are conscious beings, created with an awareness of our actions, able to make choices that aid or hinder others, the Earth, and ourselves. So often our goal is to purchase the cheapest T-shirt, for example, not knowing that the manufacturer in another country uses child labor. Would knowing make a difference to you?

Or, for expediency, we toss out all our refuse, not recycling where we can.

In November of 2002, the Prestige, an oil carrier flagged in the Bahamas, owned by the Greeks and registered in Liberia, broke in two after being towed away from the Spanish coast (which the spill has devastated.) She was holding 22 million gallons, half of which extended itself along shoreline. The rest are bubbling up from the ship nestled on the sea floor, 11,000 feet down. In 1999, the Erika oil tanker lost three million gallons off the coast of France; in 1993, the Brear divested itself of 26 million gallons in Scotland. Our own Exxon Valdez created a catastrophe in 1989 by voiding 11 million gallons into Prince William Sound in Alaska. The horrific damage done to creatures and the overall loss of quality of life could have been avoided if sufficient care was taken.

We all belong to each other. Go through life consciously. Use and develop your God given gifts of perception, compassion, and free will to help sustain other souls and the planet. You matter.

July 5, 2003

We need to be our own best friend

I recently had a conversation with friend Carmel. We were sitting at Tully's, nursing our coffee and talking about kids, community projects, faith and exhaustion, when she said something about our needing to be our own best friend. I say "something" because whatever she said after that was lost to me. Her words had hit me like a ton of bricks; a light bulb went on, however you describe making a life changing connection.

I love a lot of people. But in our discussion, it hadn't occurred to me to think of myself. When that became evident, I felt the blood rush from my head; like I'd been caught red-handed for something awful. Where was all this emotion coming from? What had we tapped into? I didn't understand my reaction, until I considered what a best friend is and does.

When I've been someone's best friend, I've been very protective and supportive. It wouldn't occur to me to make light of their difficulties, or address them disparagingly – but I do myself. I would advise them to stick up for themselves and not put up with shoddy behavior from others; tell them that they are precious, marvelous, wonderful and deserving of the best in the world – but I don't say that to myself. I would stand by them and love them through their trials, seeming failures and lapses of good judgment – but I berate myself, think less of myself; I'm not always there for me. Not like God is.

God is our best friend. At least, the God I know is.

Years ago, when I was struggling to find womankind reflected in the masculine deity I'd been trained to believe in, I saw a cartoon. It was of a preacher complaining to God on bended knee, beseeching heaven for assistance about the women in his church. In the fourth and final frame he gets his answer. A bolt of lightening comes from the sky and I read the sentence, "Just call me 'Big Mama!" I knew what I'd go through for my child; the sacrifices I would make and the love I would give. It changed my view of my Creator; made God's love accessible to me in a way I'd never experienced before. Not seeing myself reflected in the persons of the Trinity, I'd felt cut off from God. But now I saw that God is in every soul. God loved me.

What I'd disconnected from and caught myself on, that morning with Carmel, was God's unconditional love. How can I love myself any less than my Creator does? God is your own cheer leading squad; the bigger kid you hide behind on the school playground when the bullies want to pick on you. The friend you cry with on the phone or have a beer with after work when life beats you up.

Reconnecting with that understanding in a meaningful way has turned my life around. I take better care of myself now, in all ways. And it's made me a better friend, too.

July 19, 2003

Forgiveness is a way to find personal and perhaps global peace

You have many opportunities to forgive everyday, though you may not think of them that way at the time. Take for instance the child who didn't clean their room – again, or the driver who drives 5 under the speed limit. In each event, you were, to some degree, offended, angered, or otherwise upset. Usually you move through "little things" like these without much heartburn.

But then there can be times of unfathomable sorrow, disgust, or hemorrhaging rage and hate. A spouse's infidelity, or a child's murder, for example, can solicit these overwhelming emotions.

Twenty years ago, Aba Gayle's youngest daughter, Catherine, was stabbed to death by Douglas Mickey. He's still on death row in San Quentin. How she transitioned from rage and hate to forgiveness (www.catherineblountfdn.org) and friendship is nothing less than a miracle, she says.

In a telephone interview with her, she said she visited him in prison a couple weeks ago. She restated her commitment to furthering the advancement of forgiveness as a way to personal and global peace. Part of her work, she said, involved working with Robert W. Plath's "Worldwide Forgiveness Alliance" and its creation of "International Forgiveness Day" (www.forgivenessday.org).

I spoke with Plath recently and he stated that he is very gratified by the reception WFA has received and the contribution the organization is making to the growing forgiveness movement. There are three large events that he knows of and many smaller ones, he said. In the United States, California, Washington State and Hawaii (www.pioneersofforgiveness.org) lead the way, while he got a phone call from Ghana last week, telling them they would hold their first observance next month.

Think back to a time when you were consumed by the desire for revenge – to hurt someone the way you'd been hurt. Or just when all you could think of was how wounded you and/or your family was over someone's transgression against you.

I remember reading of a murder locally a few years back. Both families – those of the victim as well as the perpetrator – suffered immensely. You could see and identify with the pain in their faces as they left the courtroom. It can take distance; time away from the event for emotions to get to a point where you can work with them, instead of them working you over.

Forgiveness benefits the forgiver more than the receiver. The receiver may never know you forgave them. And forgiveness doesn't mean that you condone (www.forgivenessweb.com) or have forgotten the event. It means that you've decided not to carry the weight of all that misery any longer.

I asked co-worker Missy if she ever had anyone she had to forgive. "Oh, of course," she said. "Why did you forgive them?" "Because it was a burden I no longer wanted to carry. I did it for me."

Do it for yourself. Ask God for help. Release your burden. Free your soul from its shackle of misery and look to the Light for healing, and start really living again.

August 16, 2003

Release your negative feelings before it's too late

A friend of my best friend passed away this year. They attended their 35th high school reunion in September, and by April he was gone.

There were no symptoms to speak of; he was just a little more tired than usual. He'd recently passed a full physical, so when he went to the doctor for a minor ailment, no one expected the blood test to come back with a report indicating cancer.

We rarely know when we'll be facing the end of our days.

It is nearly impossible to live life as though you only have, say, six months to live. Your priorities shift. Money you might have been saving for that sailboat now goes toward paying off your credit cards. Or taking that trip back home to say your farewells.

Chances are you'll be examining your relationships. Do you really need to go to your grave carrying the grudges, resentments and anger you have now? What good does it do you doing that? If you could release them knowing you were dying, why don't you release them now? What's to stop you from forgiving them, and yourself? Be good to yourself and let go now.

A lot of folks facing their last days turn their attention to their creator. They want to "get right with God." Perhaps you've been avoiding contact because you're afraid of judgment and you find God unapproachable. Maybe you were turned off by some event at church, or something the pastor did or didn't do; God is so much bigger than the human beings that often represent it. It could be a tragedy in your life turned you away and you railed against God for allowing it to happen. Perhaps you grew up without any spiritual direction, but have become aware of a longing you haven't experienced before.

Why wait literally until the last minute to open the gate, cross the bridge, do whatever it takes, to connect with the source that loves you beyond our limited comprehension? The power is always "on." We just have to plug into the outlet. You have the power to allow it into your heart and soul. It's always there; you just have to let it in, turn it on.

Different faiths have different beliefs about our source. Different attributes are ascribed to "the creator of all that is seen and unseen." It is called by so many different names. Our God is an awesome God.

How is your relationship with the power that created eternity, and you?

Our lives are so incredibly busy these days. It can be difficult to carve out time to quiet yourself and tune in to the bigger picture when there are kids to feed and laundry to do, or you're in back to back meetings throughout the day. But there is absolutely no greater sustenance or reward than knowing you are thoroughly and completely loved, no matter what your circumstances.

Make a conscious union with God a priority and your whole world will change for the better.

August 30, 2003

Prayer is not limited to a specific formula

Do you pray? Where, when, how and why? Do you have a "prayer life"? Is it compartmentalized like your "family life" or "sex life"? You can't work "without ceasing", but you're admonished to pray that way, in the Bible. How is that possible? You have other things to do, like change diapers, change oil, or make change. The only way you could pray without ceasing is if your very life was a prayer; the background that your life is set into.

There are many different ways of expressing prayer, different colors, shades and degrees of it. You may not recognize that this is how it is with you because you've been trained to see things in boxes, neatly and predictably packaged. But it's possible this is how you live right now.

Its not limited to a specific formulary of words, day, or time. Your intent creates a path that opens the doors to connection and perception. Just as a parent loves a child whether they see them or not; whether they're paying the bills or out on the front lines, so it is with prayer. It can become a part of you like loving is, like breathing is; it doesn't turn off.

Paul Walsh, president of Fellowship in Prayer writes that, "when we're able to sustain (an) attitude of mindfulness toward everything we see, hear, touch and do – our whole life becomes a prayer." The activity or expression of this "being-ness" results in constant communication with God because we are not separate from God. We have a spark of divinity within us, having been created to reflect our Creator. This is what we are.

Brother David Steindl-Rast says that prayer is "simply grateful living."

This is how you can be in a state of prayerfulness anywhere, at any time. It is not confined to a group setting, or limited to a specific set of circumstances; not limited to prescribed words or even thoughts. You can pray in your chair at school, while driving a bus, or drilling a tooth. You can always be aware of your connection with God without active thought, just as you are about those you love.

Pastor Rick Warren writes in "The Purpose Driven Life" that "worship is not a part of your life, it IS your life…" This is how it is with prayer.

There are a couple opportunities for group prayer coming up soon. The first occurs on September 11th. It's Unity Church's World Day of Prayer (www.worlddayofprayer.org) In it's 10th year, it involves hundreds of churches and thousands of individuals around the world. Locally, Bremerton Unity (www.bremertonunity.org) has services and events planned.

The 18th Annual Kitsap County Prayer Breakfast will be held on Thursday, October 16th at 6:45 a.m. Held at the Red Lion Silverdale Hotel, the guest speaker is former Texas State Representative Rick Green. The cost is $15. For more information call Carl Johnson at 360-692-2945 or email him at crjoinson60@charter.net

You can pray without ceasing.

September 27, 2003

Addiction and spiritual healing

Where is God in the life of an addict?

Last week the "Washington State Meth Summit III was held in Vancouver, WA. I watched the proceedings on TVW (www.tvw.org) and listened intently as they discussed the ramifications of drug addiction on the individual, their children, families and communities.

Representatives from county after county weighed in on what they were doing to halt the terrorism addiction forces on lives. Here in Kitsap County, we have the Drug Interdiction Task Force created by Prosecuting Attorney Russ Hauge.

These are our brothers and sisters, mothers and fathers who are looking for "something" they can't find in a pipe, shot, pill, or bottom of a bottle.

The October issue of Spirituality and Health magazine (www.spiritualityhealth. com) features an article titled, "Spirituality As an Antidote For Addiction", written by William R. Miller, Ph.D, a professor of psychology and psychiatry at the University of New Mexico.

He writes, "In the language of psychology, addition is a progressive displacement of everything else in life. The addict spends increasing time with the addition (acquiring the drug, using it, recovering from its effects), and less time doing other things once valued or meaningful."

There are so many other endeavors this could apply to. It doesn't have to be a physical addiction, like meth or tobacco. It could be exercise, eating, religion, sex – anything that moves you out of balance, contributes to the "displacement" of others and other healthy behaviors.

Why doesn't God save us from ourselves?

Miller goes on to discuss the power of 12 Step programs, research on the efficacy of other spiritually-based treatments, and concludes, "Many factors, then, point to spirituality as an antidote to addiction: as a preventive, a treatment, and a path to transformation. Given the enormous suffering linked to addiction, we can scarcely afford to overlook this relatively untapped source of healing."

Rabbi Harold Kushner's latest book is titled, "The Lord is My Shepherd", and in an interview with Beliefnet (www.beliefnet.com) he states, "…God's promise was never that life would be fair. God's promise was that when we have to confront the unfairness of life, we will be able to handle it because we won't do it alone – He'll be with us."

He continues, "A naïve conception of God is a God who is always there to protect us. We replace it with a more realistic understanding of a God who is there to help us through the difficult times in our lives. The psalmist doesn't say, 'I will fear no evil because nothing bad ever happens in the world.' He says, 'I will fear no evil because it doesn't scare me because God is with me.'"

Friend Sky tells me we often medicate our sufferings when we are separate from God. The love of God is always present, but we become disconnected when we are living in darkness without God's guiding light. "When our whole being becomes our prayer, we are reconnected to our spiritual source."

October 11, 2003

For many, ethics are driven by religious morals. Are yours?

Do you consider yourself an ethical person? What makes you think so?

The Merriam-Webster Dictionary On-Line defines "ethic" as "The discipline dealing with what is good and bad and with moral duty and obligation." Also, "The principles of conduct governing an individual or group."

How do you know if yours are good or bad? Does it matter to you?

"By their fruits we will know them."

For many, ethics are driven by religious morals and values. You can, however, be a religious person with bad ethics, and an atheist with good ethics. Believing in a deity does not automatically make you think or act in an ethical manner.

Enron experienced a "broad systemic failure" because they (corporate leaders) behaved unethically. They lied, cheated and stole from consumers and employees. They misrepresented themselves and were greedy. They did not treat others with respect, honesty, or fairness.

We bring our ethics to the workplace. You can have an unethical employer, and still be true to your beliefs. Sometimes you can do it and not risk your job; you pick your battles. Other times you must weigh the consequences: keep your mouth shut and not rock the boat, or speak up and risk losing the house. In my 30+ years of employment, this has happened a couple times.

What are your personal criteria for ethical behavior? How are they tied in to your religious beliefs? How closely do you live them out?

One of the most widely read statements on business ethics is the 4-Way Test created by Rotarian Herbert Taylor. It asks four questions:

"Of the things we think, say, or do, 1. Is it the TRUTH? 2. Is it FAIR to all concerned? 3. Will it build GOODWILL and BETTER FRIENDSHIPS? 4. Will it be BENEFICIAL to all concerned?"

Try holding this as your personal ethic for a week. All four have to apply to all situations. Be aware of how you talk to and treat the kids, friends, co-workers, congregants and customers. Is there room for improvement?

If you're a Christian, chances are you look to Jesus as a role model for your life. You ask yourself, "What would Jesus do?"

What WOULD Jesus do? He isn't around physically to ask questions of, and society today is fraught with questions we didn't have before. We struggle with issues like cloning, sexuality and the Pledge of Allegiance.

Different faiths offer different perspectives, yet most have a common theme of "treat others as you would like to be treated."

Meg Ryan hosts a 12-minute video funded by the Kellogg and Mott Foundations, designed specifically to "help young people examine their personal ethics. It demonstrates effective techniques for finding one's personal values and standards, and presents some very striking examples of what can happen when people don't search inside themselves. It allows viewers to understand and articulate their own personal ethics and their ethical standards." You can find more info at www.customflix.com/Store/Show/Ttl.jsp?id=204553

Our ethics can change a neighborhood or a nation. Please give some thought to yours.

October 25, 2003

What does your soul mean to you and how do you feed it?

What is a soul and how do you care for it?

The best description I've come across for "soul" is that it is that invisible part of you that is your connection to God; to the divine. While it has to do with things eternal, it also has to do with your humanity; with the quality of your life, and how you relate to yourself and others. Everyone has a soul whether they consider themselves "religious" or not. It comes with the body.

How do you feed your soul?

I was watching the National Geographic channel's program on how photography has changed our lives, when the thought occurred to me, "This feeds my soul!" I then spent the rest of the day figuring out what that meant to me.

What I revel in is seeing the miracle of life in slow motion. Becoming intimate with the birth and death of starlings and stars, worms and whales. Observing the web of life and our inter connectedness with the universe. The glory of God revealed by nanotechnology. It fills my spirit to overflowing, and I am again awe struck by the handiwork of the Creator.

Feeding your soul is more than just what makes you feel "good." Buying a rump roast on sale can make you feel good. It helps to be conscious of the fact that you are a soul first, here on a mission. When you work to meet the goals of your mission, you feed your soul. You don't have to be "religious" for this to happen, or doing something overtly spiritual. God is in your life whether you acknowledge its presence or not.

Food for the soul could be those experiences that help you understand and strengthen your connection or communion with God. You may not be aware that this is what is happening, if God's presence isn't visible to you. Yet the Creator is not absent from creation.

Jesus said (paraphrased) whatever you do for others you do for me (Mt. 25:36-40). God is within and without at the same time, as air is. If it isn't throughout a body, it dies. We cannot live without oxygen and that is what the love of God is for many. The good you do for others turns out to be the good you do for yourself.

I have several friends who do missionary work in other countries, and other friends who help out at disasters in this country. This feeds their souls.

My mother used to write musicals and concertos. Friend Carmel facilitates a weekly spirituality group, and Missy is working towards participation in a triathlon. Another provides hospice care. It's different things for different people.

Raise your awareness of the beauty of the world around you. Express gratitude for what you are and what you have. Tell those you care about how much they mean to you.

Devote some time this week to the care and maintenance of your relationship with God. It's good food for your soul.

November 8, 2003

40 days, 40 nights – number important to many

The number 40 has significance in many religions.

For the Jewish, for example, according to the Torah, Moses ascended Mt. Sinai three times (www.aish.com) to receive the 10 Commandments twice, spending 40 days each time. The rain fell 40 days for Noah in the ark. And the Jewish people wandered 40 years in the desert.

For the Muslim, in the Qur'an, there are numerous examples of the number, which indicates change from one state or way of being, to another (www.pakistanlink.com).

In Christianity, Jesus spent 40 days in the desert fasting and praying, perhaps reflecting on his mission in life and his commitment to its purpose. We know, too, that it was a time of testing, of trial. He was confronted by temptations that would have him reject what he knew himself to be; what he knew he had to do.

Jesus was tempted to use his abilities and gifts for his own gain; to go for instant gratification of his wants and needs. He stayed faithful to his call, even through his death and resurrection. Many celebrate the Ascension, which falls 40 days after Easter.

These days, 40 days is playing a very large part of many lives. At Amazon.com there are literally dozens of books on the subject, offering personal retreats and meditations for searching souls.

Rev. Mary Manin Morrissey, whose church, "Living Enrichment Center" in Wilsonville, OR is doing a "40 Days of Purpose" program, states that 40 days "is a spiritually significant time…for true transformation."

What has the country talking, however, is Pastor Rick Warren's book, "The Purpose Driven Life" which spent 23 weeks on The New York Times best-seller list and months on USA TODAY'S Best Selling Books list. Christianity Today has called him, "America's most influential pastor." The evangelist is part of the Southern Baptist Convention.

Throughout its 40 chapters, the book calls you to "become what God created you to be", and focuses on a program of worship, study, fellowship and service.

On the website, www.purposedriven.com, a search states that 163 churches in Washington state are participating in the "40 Days of Purpose" campaign.

Why is the book so popular? Because it meets an unmet need for many … the need to know the meaning of life, the reason for their existence.

Ralph Waldo Emerson wrote, "What lies behind us and what lies before us are tiny matters compared to what lies within us."

Whether you choose to utilize this book or another, it's a good time of year to take stock of your life. I know that recent events have caused deep reflection on how I'm living my life. Our time on this planet is limited. I've been asking myself, "Am I just getting by or am I living my life to its fullest potential? Am I stretching out of my comfort zone to help others?"

The Sufi poet, Rumi states, "What nine months in the womb does for the embryo, so 40 days of spiritual focus will do for you."

Begin now.

November 22, 2003

Nothing's better than thankfulness

I can't remember a time in my life when I've been more thankful to be alive. While I'm an introspective semi-introvert at heart, I have never given it as much thought as I have lately.

I have two dear friends with inoperable, terminal cancer.

The emotions that flood your body unbidden, as a witness to this diagnosis, are almost incomprehensible. Being close to one of them on an almost daily basis, seeing the shock and tears and courage, has absolutely changed my life. Considering what they must be considering now has me weighing my decisions and experiences differently.

I cry because I love them and will miss the presence of such wise souls in my life. I will miss their smiles, laughter, and hugs.

I cry because they do, over the anticipated loss of control, loved ones, and opportunities.

Even having faith in God and belief in the afterlife, the human condition – our mortality – calls most of us to respond initially with some measure of fear. You are going into the unknown with your eyes wide open, with time to speculate on the worst, or the best, that the future holds.

When you think you've got 20, 30 or 50 years to live, you do life differently than you would if you knew the end of your physical existence was mere months away. Are you under-living your life?

What are you thankful for?

I am thankful for the love of my son. It has sustained me through my darkest hours and brought light and joy into every day.

I am thankful for the love of my friends and family. I mean this seriously because often times I give them reason not to.

I am thankful for the doctors that have extended the quality and length of my life, the authors of the books I treasure, and the music that fills my soul.

I am thankful to The Sun and my editor for allowing us to journey together.

I am thankful for our gray skies, rain, and the seagulls that leave deposits on the hood of my truck. It means I am still able to walk and drive, see and smell my beloved Puget Sound.

I am thankful for the scientists and theologians who have filled my mind with thoughts and questions; who have helped me behold, with awe, the wonder of our galaxy, quantum physics, plum trees, manatees, love, mercy and compassion, and all things that I ponder.

What are you thankful for?

Sunrises and sunsets in purple and gold, hovering just over the top of the trees? The gurgle of your infant granddaughter? The fire fighters who risked their lives to save your home?

I am thankful that I can acknowledge the presence and love of the Creator. That I can sit in silence with the love of my life, my God, knowing that my friends are just leaving their physical forms and going back to their original one – spirit. Out of sight, but never out of my heart.

What are you thankful for?

December 6, 2003

No denomination has all the answers, but they can each point the right way

I really enjoyed reading Scripps Howard News Service religion writer David Water's column of October 22nd titled, "Christ has plenty of room for divisions" (www.knoxstudio.com/shns/story.cfm?pk=faith-faith-10-22-03&cat=lr).

He focused on the merits of multiple expressions of Christianity and states that, according to "the World Christian Encyclopedia, there are more than 20,800 Christian denominations."

Waters writes, "I used to think the continuous fragmenting of the Body of Christ was a bad thing. That lack of unity in the church showed lack of loyalty to Christ. That dissent eventually would spell disaster for the church. No doubt, disagreement among Christians turns many people away from the church. Still, as there are more denominations than ever, there are more Christians than ever."

He continues, "Just about every breakup within the church, no matter how senseless or painful, gives a lot of people more breathing room. More room to stop fussing and fighting with one another over what John Wesley (the Anglican who founded Methodism) called 'nonessentials' – man made rules and regulations that govern denominations."

There is more that unites us than separates us.

In July of 2004, the World Parliament of Religions meets in Spain (www.cpwr. org). From the website we read that, "The mission of the Council for a Parliament of the World's Religions is to cultivate harmony between the world's religious and spiritual communities and foster their engagement with the world and its other guiding institutions in order to achieve a peaceful, just, and sustainable world."

Over the years, my perspective on faith and religion has morphed significantly. I grew up in a faith that taught it was their way or the highway to hell. That is so not "me" anymore. My direction to change came from the Bible.

We read that Jesus was asked, "Teacher, which is the greatest commandment in the law?" To which he replied, "Love the Lord your God with all your heart, soul, and mind. The second is like it: Love your neighbor as yourself."

Christianity, like other religions, is a Spirit inspired construct of humanity. It did not exist at the time Jesus is reported to have spoken the words above.

Marcus Borg recently spoke at St. Mark's Episcopal Cathedral in Seattle. Theologian, professor, and author of best sellers, Jesus: A New Vision and Meeting Jesus Again for the First Time, he spoke on his latest book, The Heart of Christianity: Rediscovering A Life of Faith.

In it he writes, "Each of the enduring religions is a mediator of 'the absolute,' but not 'absolute' itself. Applying this understanding to being Christian, the point is not to believe that Christianity as the only absolute and adequate revelation of God. Rather, the point is to live within the Christian tradition as a sacrament of the sacred, a mediator of the absolute, whom we name 'God' and who for us is known decisively in Jesus. Christianity is not absolute, but points to and mediates the absolute."

The Absolute, the Light, the Creator, God.

December 20, 2003

To buy numerous gifts or celebrate the Lord's birth? What would Jesus do?

I'm having trouble getting into the holiday mood this year. I'm turned off by the commercialism; even religious and spiritual folk buy into it.

I remember as a kid, my mom telling me that purchasing gifts at Christmas (which she couldn't afford in the dead of December when even I knew we had to pay higher heating bills) represented the gift that Jesus was to us. But there was so much more to it. It seemed like how many you had and the brand name meant something, too, to the kids at school. And no one ever connected the gift of Jesus with the one under the tree. So why do we do this every year? How does what we put ourselves through now honor Jesus or benefit Christianity?

I think we should set a different date to celebrate Jesus the Christ's birth date and let the shoppers have December 25th.

Why do people go into debt for this? Is this what Jesus would do? Is this how you think he'd want to have the day of his birth remembered?

In order to get a clue as to what kind of remembrance Jesus might prefer, we need to examine what his priorities and values were, how he lived his life, and the decisions he made.

- Jesus prayed anywhere - in a temple or out in nature, walking along the road or before a meal.
- He lived a simple life. When offered the temptation of worldly, material goods, he turned away. We embrace it. Bigger, more elaborate homes and places of worship with intricate security systems to protect them. Jesus owned nothing but the clothes on his back. What extra he had he gave to others. I'm not advocating everyone become homeless, itinerant preachers – that's a specific calling in life. But we sure can do a whole lot better of sharing than we do now.
- He hung out with outcasts. Those on the periphery of acceptable society he drew to him. We exclude so many people with our thoughts and behavior when we could be influencing them toward a better, more holy life by our loving example of acceptance. Mother Teresa told us over and over, by word and deed, that Christ is among us in the worst disguises. Jesus said that when we care for those in need, those that are homeless, in prison, in nursing homes; when we advocate for the defenseless and right wrongs, we do it to him. We don't do that by isolating ourselves in our own little cocoons of living with only a passing thought for the needs of others.

There is a lot of good done at Christmas, too. A lot of folks have the right idea and live with the love of Jesus in their hearts all year long. But if it is our intention to honor Christ with this holiday, then we need to turn it out from ourselves, and direct it to those in need.

2004

January 3, 2004

Books and Web sites worth a look

This is my annual column with recommendations for books and Web sites that I've found to be stimulating, insightful, provocative or otherwise worth checking out. Some were new to me this year, are old favorites, or have been recommended by friends I trust. Whenever possible, I'll check the book out from the library. If the desire to underline or highlight is overwhelming, I'll go buy it.

My favorite new book this year was "Thinking For A Change" by John C. Maxwell. I liked it so much I bought copies for friends. It was invigorating and inspirational. Had to highlight!

Right behind it were two recommended by my friend Carmel. The first is a daily reader, "Words To Live By" by Ecknath Easwaran (she even bought me the book). The second I purposely avoided reading (I didn't like the title) until Carmel asked me to give it a chance. It is "How to Know God" by Deepak Chopra. I'm only a third of the way through it and am enjoying it immensely.

For the first time I have a couple authors with more than one book I want to mention. The first is Edward Hays, one of the all time greatest spiritual storytellers I've encountered. I've recommended his "St. George and the Dragon" in past years, and am reading "Prayer Notes to a Friend" and "The Ladder" now. They are thought provoking and inspirational.

The second is Eckhart Tolle. His first book, "The Power of Now" literally changed my life for the better, although it was a hard read for me. There were times a paragraph would set me back for a week to digest and comprehend. His latest, "Stillness Speaks", is like a condensed "The Power of Now" in sound bites. It reinforces "Now". I like it a lot.

The third is John C. Maxwell. Along with the first book I mentioned, I'm also reading his "There's No Such Thing as Business Ethics." He hits the nail on the head. It's good reading for everyone.

Other books I'm reading are "The Art of Happiness at Work" by HH The Dalai Lama (I usually read it during my lunch break), "A Walk With Four Spiritual Guides" by Andrew Harvey, and "Spiritual Innovators" by Ira Rifkin. All are excellent reading. Next in line to be read are "The Heart of Christianity" by Marcus Borg, "Crones Don't Whine" by Jean Shinoda Bolen, and a referral from friend Sky, "Passionate Presence" by Catherine Ingram. I'm excited about '04 already!

Favorites I'd like to mention are "Wilderness Spirituality" by Rod Romney, "The Ecstatic Journey" by Sophy Burnham, and "The Mystic Vision", compiled by Andrew Harvey.

I encourage you, too, to read the sacred works of your faith.

There were a couple websites that I visited frequently this year, too. Besides previously recommended www.beliefnet.org and www.spiritualityhealth.com, I'm adding www.interfaithcouncil.com and www.cpwr.org (Council for a Parliament of World Religions).

These are all food for the journey. Enjoy!

January 17, 2004

Celebrate the everyday heroes around you

What makes someone a "hero"?

Our local chapter of the Red Cross is asking folks to submit nominations on local heroes – people who have displayed "extraordinary acts of courage or kindness" – so they can be recognized at their "Real Heroes Breakfast."

We need more events like this to draw attention to the pervasive goodness in our communities. So much news centers on things we collectively think of as "bad", with only a passing glimpse (or so it may seem) given to that, which is positive and uplifting.

This newspaper, The Sun (out of Bremerton, WA) publishes their "Neighbors" section every week. Its purpose is to emphasize this very issue. It's all about the high notes: folks serving in the military, family reunions, graduations, acts of kindness, promotions, etc. It's just wonderful, and I wish doing this sort of thing was more commonplace. It's what we need more of.

Heroes are everywhere.

From the teachers who fund class supplies from their paychecks to the firefighter who carries a dad from his burning home, good people and good acts are everywhere. And because they are, it can be easy to overlook them.

There are many acts of heroism that aren't visible at all. Quiet decisions that are made in someone's heart to forgive, for example, or to place someone else's needs above their own.

Where does courage like this come from? Not everyone relies on God for it. Some folks aren't religious or spiritually aware at all yet they show great love and compassion for others.

In the Bible we read that humanity is made in the image and likeness of the Creator. So whether you operate consciously of it or not, it is still the core of "you." As Carl Jung wrote, "Bidden or not bidden, God is present."

Male or female, no matter the race, color or creed, the essential essence of you, or your soul, is of God. Even those who have committed the most heinous crimes have this in common with saints; they have just chosen to ignore the call.

While we wouldn't want to be unaware of the painful realities of this world, we can certainly focus more on what we want to grow: peace, hope, and prosperity for all souls. It can be a matter of just changing the orientation of a situation. Instead of focusing on poor health, for example, focus on becoming healthier. Instead of paying attention to what you don't have, focus on what you do and give thanks for that.

You may not see yourself this way - you may focus on your shortcomings instead of your strengths, but which do you want to prosper? If you're a Christian you believe Jesus the Christ made the supreme sacrifice for you. He is your hero. What better way to honor him than to live a life that loves God with all you are and your neighbor as yourself.

January 31, 2004

We must never forget the fallen soldiers in Iraq

My brother, Chet, came home from the Vietnam War a changed man. There is no way you can be exposed to and engage in such violent activity and not find the way you relate to yourself, community, and world, altered in some way.

These days he finds himself sitting on his front porch listening to classical music and news radio. His friend, Lee, also a vet, crosses the quiet street they live on to join him on the porch, and they chat. Sometimes quite loudly, Chet tells me, when it comes to the state of our country.

His voice rising, frustration and anger clear in his tone, he told me in a phone call how incomprehensible it is to him that no one running for president in '04, the media, local communities – no one – is raising a stink about all the kids that are dying every day in Iraq.

"I'm watching all these politicians on TV and not one of them is screaming about all those dads and sons, brothers and sisters that have died and continue to die over there. These guys who are trying to win us veterans over - where are the names of these people? They're dropping like flies every day and no one is yelling about how terrible that is. Why aren't we making a bigger effort to bring everybody home? Why isn't it at the top of everyone's agenda? Is life cheap? Even those who feel their kids died for a good reason have to be hurting. What are we doing to help them cope? Why isn't anybody screaming about this? Didn't God create everybody's children?"

His heated delivery convicted me. When was the last time I had given them a second thought? Done something to help a family, even if all I could do was remember them in my prayers? Out of sight, out of mind – the war is "over there" unless your beloved is.

I understand that no one person can correct all the inequities in the world. But surely, each one of us can do something in our corner of it. How can we love our neighbor as our self in this situation?

Spiritual mentor and friend, the Rev. Dr. Rodney Romney writes, "We can no longer submerge ourselves in a pious patriotism that sees our nation as the only one God blesses or cares about. It is the world God loves. We can love our country and be grateful for its legacy of freedom, but we must not let this love cut us off from others who have a different heritage. We are, at least temporarily, all citizens of the one world in which we now live."

We're so comfortable in our routines and "business as usual" lives. But what if it was our child being shipped out? What if it was our husband with a broken heart, kissing the kids goodbye, looking back just one more time to freeze the memory in place?

We cannot ignore or forget them. They are us.

February 14, 2004

Lent is a time to look for answers and introspection

I love the season of Lent. To my way of thinking, I live it every day. You can appreciate it no matter your religious affiliation. The forty day period before Easter, it begins this year on February 25 and ends April 10 (you don't count the Sundays.)

I grew up in the Roman Catholic tradition, in a Polish household. We ate fish on Friday, wore what us little girls called "doilies" on our heads, and went to Confession every Saturday whether we had anything to confess or not. My mom, like most moms in our neighborhood, felt it couldn't hurt. Attending Catholic school, Sister Maria taught me piano in the rectory on Wednesdays. It was short lived, as I couldn't reach an octave.

Every school day we attended Mass before classes started. I ate my peanut butter and jelly sandwich during our first period, as did most of the other kids. Between daily Mass, school, and Sunday service, a lot of time was spent on the subject of God: Father, Son, and Holy Ghost, and the traditions and the seasons of the Church.

I loved Lent more than Christmas; my mother said that was odd for a child. But I've always loved looking for answers, and going inside myself has never scared me. I always felt God was there if I needed help confronting or accepting anything I discovered.

Lent, to me, is primarily a time of introspection. Of taking stock of your life and seeing what worked and what didn't. The Church adds the dimension of repentance as part of the preparation for Easter, for Jesus' resurrection. It was always a very sober, solemn time of year.

Giving up something for Lent, or denying yourself something you enjoy as a means of sharing in the suffering of Christ, was very important. As a family, one year, we decided we would skip our Sunday outing for ice cream. This had the added benefit of saving my stepfather a lot of money.

"Giving up something" was the rule until I was in my early 30's and the pastor of the church I was attending turned my world around. He said, "Instead of taking away something, add something. If the goal is to prepare your soul to receive Christ anew, do something for others you wouldn't ordinarily do. And it can't be as easy as mailing a check. Carve time out from your busy schedule to read for the blind at the library. Or visit a nursing home and help braid someone's hair. See if there are any soup kitchens that need someone to chop carrots. Jesus has no other hands, now, but yours. Do it for Jesus."

What can you do this Lenten season to enhance your relationship with your Creator? How can you be Jesus for someone? "For I was hungry and you fed me, thirsty and you gave me drink. In prison and you visited me."

You are so talented, with so much love and compassion to share. Find a way.

February 28, 2004

64 days of nonviolence give opportunity to reflect

The 2004 "Season for Nonviolence" (www.season-for-nonviolence.net and www.agnt.org) began January 30 and ends April 4. These 64 days encompass the time between the assassination of Mohandas "Mahatma" Gandhi, and the Rev. Dr. Martin Luther King, Jr. Endorsed and supported by the families of these peacemakers, this "season" gives us an opportunity to listen and think hard about what they truly mean to us.

We revere their names. We believe in what they gave their lives for. Or do we? Do we pay lip service to their causes but in our heart feel their goals are unobtainable; too "pie in the sky"? Does nonviolence apply to all of life or only part of it? What do we teach our children (if anything) about nonviolence? That it's OK to blast someone's brains out on a video screen but not in school? This is uncomfortable territory, I know, but take a look at whether or not in your daily living there is a disconnect between your beliefs and your actions.

Is it always someone else who starts the violence and you're merely responding in kind?

Violence isn't limited to physical wounding. Violence is thoughts and words, intentions and glances that inflict pain on another, or on one's self. Most of the hunger and poor health in the world is a by-product of a form of violence.

In his acceptance speech for the Nobel Peace Prize in 1964, Dr. King stated, "Nonviolence is the answer to the crucial political and moral questions of our time;

the need for man to overcome oppression and violence without resorting to oppression and violence. Man must evolve for all human conflict a method which rejects revenge, aggression and retaliation. The foundation of such a method is love."

The Very Reverend Robert V. Taylor of St. Mark's Cathedral in Seattle (www. saintmarks.org), in his February 15 sermon recounts an experience he had recently in Jerusalem, watching the "separation barrier" being built. The structure, 403 miles long and 25 feet high, is intended to provide protection for the Israelis from suicide bombings and other violence. It also includes electrified fencing and sniper towers.

"(Peace) never happens because of any walls that we create," he stated. "It happens when we commit to the work of bringing people with different narratives together to speak truth, to grow trust, and to imagine that which God already knows: that we are deeply related to one another."

In his newest book, "God Has a Dream", Desmond Tutu states, "...every 3.6 seconds someone dies of hunger and three quarters of these are children under five. If we realized that we are family, we would not let this happen."

Gandhi wrote, "We may never be strong enough to be entirely nonviolent in thought, word and deed. But we must keep nonviolence as our goal and make strong progress towards it."

Violence kills bodies, minds and spirits in so many ways. If everyone worked to eliminate it from their families and neighborhoods, we would see the transformation of the world.

March 13, 2004

Children pay a price for their parents' mistakes

Girl Scouts Beyond Bars is a national program that works to develop and maintain loving connections between incarcerated women and their daughters. Studies have shown that there is a higher incidence of at-risk behavior, such as teen pregnancy and truancy, in the children of those behind bars than those that aren't.

Children pay the price of a parent's errors in their own way. They are behind different bars, and can grow up to replicate their parent's lives if something doesn't intervene to show a different way of dealing with the "stuff" of life. This is where organizations like the Girl and Boy Scouts can do so much to give a child a healthy sense of belonging, provide positive examples, and hope for the future.

It's bad enough when a parent leaves the family unit for any length of time under good circumstances. Imagine what it must be like to be a child and see your mom or dad arrested, placed into handcuffs, and taken away. Imagine the grief and tears, the embarrassment at school and church. If the parent doing time was the only one in the home, imagine the upheaval in the child's life as they go into foster care, or be taken in by family members. Perhaps there is a change in schools, causing further isolation, alienation and stress.

There could be unresolved anger at the parent for making a choice that took them away; anger at having to grow up too fast. Not caring what happens and having nothing to lose or (seemingly) live for, self-defeating attitudes can take over and risky behaviors ensue. And another precious child of God faces the edge.

Seal's song, "Love's Divine", is profound. He sings, "Give me love, love is what I need to help me know my name." If a person truly knew who walked within them, if they knew their true identity of being made in the image of their Creator, in their hearts as well as their heads, there would be no drug use; no burglary or prostitution to support drug use. No meth labs with toxic fumes and chemicals for anyone to take in to their bodies and suffer for years to come.

Love of self is not a dirty word. For how can you "love your neighbor as yourself" if you don't understand that the spirit of God resides in each soul? You must nurture and respect and provide discipline for yourself just as you would your child. They shouldn't have to live without the love and encouragement that comes from a parent fully present, fully alive.

In the absence of loving parent(s), or in addition to, thank God for the scouts.

Locally, GSBB was established at the Washington Corrections Center for Women in Purdy in 1999. There are approximately 65 girls and 50 inmates participating at the present time, with plans to develop a "Boy Scouts Beyond Bars" program this year. It will be the first of its kind in the nation.

March 27, 2004

Reach out and listen to troubled youth

On March 18, 2004, in the small town of Joyce, a 13-year old youth carried in to school his books and guitar case. He sat at the back of a class, removed a rifle from the case, and shot and killed himself.

By all accounts, he was a well-adjusted child. The day after, his family was still trying to find out why he did it. No suicide note has been found as yet. Yet there had to be a reason.

Suicide is a permanent solution to a temporary problem, my mother used to say. She had considered it several times as a means of finally escaping from the family violence and abuse that haunted her. Even when the years of emotional, physical and sexual abuse had ended, she was left with her memories and worries for the safety of her three daughters.

Chances are it has crossed your mind, even fleetingly, or you know someone who has struggled with it. The desire to get away from pain can be overwhelming. There are many curves in the road; what if you just drove straight?

Behind accidents and homicides, suicide among those 15 to 25 years of age is the third leading cause of death. The third leading cause of death! Wouldn't something of this magnitude be considered an epidemic? What are we missing that so many of our beloveds believe there is insufficient reason to persevere with life?

People of faith take their lives, just as those of no faith tradition do. Are we limited to "after the fact" consolation of the family? What does this say about our ability to give kids the understanding that each one is a blessing? That they never go through tough times alone? The sad fact, though, is that many do. They feel something they've done, or are, is unforgivable or unacceptable. Or they can't see a light at the end of their particular tunnel and the train fills their vision.

Good Charlotte, in their song, "Hold On", sings, "This world is cold. But you don' have to go. You're feeling sad, you're feeling lonely, and no one seems to care. But we all bleed the same way as you do, and we all have the same things to go through. Hold on, if you feel like letting go. Hold on, it gets better than you know. Your days are way too long, and your nights, you can't sleep at all. And you're not sure what you're waiting for, or looking for, but you don't want to no more. Hold on."

Faith organizations can help by making sure there are no marginalized children among them. By encouraging their youth to bring friends to events, and then making them welcome, no matter their parents income, how they dress, their demeanor or scent. Would Jesus reject anyone because of appearances? We know for a fact that he would not. The outer look may not be appealing, but "we all bleed the same."

Reach out and listen.

April 10, 2004

Celebrate yourself this Sunday

Tomorrow is Easter Sunday. Across the planet, Christians will be celebrating an event that changed the world. While millions through the course of human history have been tortured in the worst imaginable ways – and still are today – the thing about Jesus is that it is believed he rose from the dead and was seen by others. He appeared on the road to Emmaus and walked awhile with two friends who, we read in Luke 24, were "kept" from recognizing him. He materialized in an upper room with disciples where the door was locked. And were told his body physically ascended into the heavens.

On this walk into town, and later at dinner, the risen Jesus laid it all out for them.

Spoke about how the Son of Man had to suffer, had to die, had to come back from the dead. It was all in The Plan. It was all meant to be.

No one is to blame for Jesus' death if it was all in God's plan. Right? Even those who did "wrong" – betraying, judging, torturing and killing the body of Jesus – were unknowingly working together for good. How else could it be if it was part of The Plan?

Jesus went into the desert and was tempted to turn away from The Plan and live the high life. Can't you just hear that angel saying, "You know what's ahead. You know what they're going to do to you. You don't have to go that route. You have the power to take the easy way out. Here, turn this stone into bread. Better yet, forget about what you came here to do, create some denari and get some new threads."

You have a plan, too, but it can be hard to embrace and live out. You face the same types of temptations as Jesus did. And have the same strength to call upon. Christians are called on to forever ask themselves, based on their understanding of his life, "What would Jesus do?" because it's the gold standard for living.

When asked what the number one law for living was, he said it is to love God with all you are, and your neighbor as yourself. Do your decisions support that goal? Are you tenaciously holding on to memories (because once something happens, that's what they are) of anger, resentment and hate? Do you, the forgiven, withhold forgiveness from others? Or do you seek to give to others the love, compassion, understanding and solace you believe Jesus gave to you?

Many are waiting for Jesus to return. I think maybe he's already here. He comforts and supports those who are hanging on to life by their fingernails, and those who struggle to stop smoking anything. He's with the mom who can't get the baby to stop crying and the soldier who was blown to bits by a shoulder held rocket launcher. He's with you. Or he can be with you, if you let him.

What will you choose this day?

April 24, 2004

Sometimes I wonder;
what is a good Christian to do?

It's always troubled me that many of us who call ourselves Christian, and who claim to ardently emulate the decisions and actions of Jesus the Christ, so often brutalize our brothers and sisters by acts of omission or commission.

What one country claims is self-defense the other does, too. One country says it's merely paying back the other for what they did, and the other country says that's what they did, too. It will never end if someone doesn't just STOP.

Yet when one country is attacked by another, whether or not they have declared "Christian leadership", what are they to do? Certainly you can't let the abuser think they got away with hurting you. There must be retribution for what they've done, too. They don't hold to the same standards you do, therefore you must respond at their level. What is a good Christian to do?

If only they (whomever "they" are) would see things our way, do things the way we want, there would be no problems. If only your boss paid you a living wage, you wouldn't have to steal from the storeroom. If only your husband paid more attention to you, you wouldn't have to flirt with another woman's husband. If only your parents were reasonable, you wouldn't have to sneak out to party. If only you were from the right tribe / race / religion / political preference / gender / age / size ...

Just as we condemn child and elder abuse, rape and murder, we must learn to be intolerant of prejudice, violence, retribution and hatred. They must be replaced with love, compassion, forgiveness, equity and tolerance. If they aren't, aren't we doomed to repeat the great horrors of our past?

April 18th was Yom Ha'Sho'ah, or Holocaust Remembrance Day. It marks a very dark day in our history when people who thought they were doing the right thing murdered over four million other people. We didn't learn from our past and it happened again, in Rwanda, Cambodia and Iraq. Fear kept someone from standing up and saying, "No. I won't participate in this."

Do you remember the poem written during WWII by Rev. Martin Niemoller? It read, "First they came for the Communists, and I didn't speak up because I wasn't one. Then they came for the Jews, and I didn't speak up because I wasn't a Jew. Then they came for the Catholics, and I didn't speak up because I was a Protestant. Then they came for me, and by that time there was no one left to speak up for me."

We could constantly change the words to fit the crimes, but when will it end? How do we resolve crises like these without adding to them with more killing? How do we defend others and stand in the gap if we don't perpetuate the problem?

So often we use God as the bully club. We need to make sure God isn't our excuse for our exercising a lack of patience, diplomacy, advocacy, and yes, love.

May 8, 2004

Officers stand in the gap for us; now is the time to honor that

The concept and action of "standing in the gap" comes from Ezekiel. In broad terms, it means to "be there", or intercede on behalf of a person or group. To stand in the gap means to be a bridge between what someone has and needs.

This is the gift our peace officers give us everyday. It is a gift because there is no possible monetary compensation equivalent to that of a life, even though we try.

Every day they stand in the gap for our communities, providing protection, strength and inspiration.

Every day they report for duty, there is a higher than average chance they may not return home after their shift.

Every day, they and their families try to cope with the tension and stress that arise from a loved one possibly responding to a domestic violence call; a bank robbery; a meth lab.

Research shows that the divorce rate for law enforcement is higher than the national average of 50%. Continued high stress often causes an immune system to break down. Maintaining a healthy family life can be very difficult.

Sure, a shift may not require an officer to release their weapon or chase a vehicle at high speeds...but they don't know that when they buckle on their belt to go to work.

To lose an officer in the line of duty leaves an open wound in their community.

On Wednesday, May 12, at 7 p.m. there will be a Peace Officer's Memorial Service at Christian Life Center in Port Orchard. Everyone is invited to attend.

Please come. It's an opportunity for you to show your support of these everyday heroes; these souls that truly love their neighbors as themselves.

If you wish there was a way to stand in the gap for them while they do for you, there is.

Bremerton Police Department Officer and Chaplain Ken Butler began an Adopt-A-Cop ministry in our area earlier this year. After explaining the goals and process to the pastor and congregation of a church, he offers them the opportunity to adopt an officer. The officer would have already agreed to participate.

Officer Butler says, "While a bullet proof vest affords a certain level of protection for our police officers, an even greater shield of protection can be found in the power of a faithful, praying church."

Thus far he has 12 churches signed up. If you'd like more details on this ministry, you can contact Officer Butler at (360) 473-5218.

According to the "Washington State Law Enforcement Memorial and 1099 (Officer Needs Assistance code) Foundation", 275 officers have lost their lives in the line of duty since 1853. Between Kitsap, Mason, Clallam, and Jefferson counties, nine officers have died. In the Washington State Patrol alone, 22 have perished.

If you aren't affiliated with a church but would like to pray for an officer, pray for one you know or for the chief of police and/or sheriff in your area. Their responsibilities are great, requiring wisdom, patience and dedication.

May 22, 2004

No moral high ground in violence

I believe that there are no circumstances that justify torture.

"You're not responsible for the security of a nation, either," you may say. True. But what does it say about a society that condones and uses it?

In an article in the May 14, 2004 Seattle Times, guest columnist Darius Rejali, author of the book "Torture and Democracy", outlines the extent and types of torture that are used in our world. It's on the Web; please read it.

He writes, "In 1956 the CIA commissioned two experts...who described the effects of forced standing. The ankles and feet swell to twice their normal size within 24 hours. Moving becomes agony. Large blisters develop. The heart rate increases and some faint. The kidneys eventually shut down.

In the 1920's, he says, forced standing was "a routine police torture in America." My America? Home of the free and the brave?

The South African and Brazilian police made prisoners stand on cans or bricks, the edges causing excruciating pain. In 1999 the South African Truth Commission determined that forced standing (used to sound innocuous, didn't it? After all, they do it voluntarily on Survivor) was the third most common torture during apartheid, after beating and applying electricity."

The jolts of electricity would make the hooded victims feet stick to the cans and force them to stand up straight.

This particular technique of torture, we learn, is called "the Vietnam"; American and South Vietnamese interrogators using field phone batteries commonly used it.

For those who think the end justifies the means, is that just supposed to work to our advantage? We call them barbaric; they call us the same thing.

Our actions speak louder than our words.

We've been torturing folks we needed something from for ages, it would appear, to one degree or another, yet we make it sound like we own the moral high ground. A line from Matthew 7 crossed my mind. It reads, "...first take the log out of your own eye, and then you will see clearly to take the speck out of your brother's eye." (ESV)

If you believe in a loving, compassionate, forgiving deity, how do you square this behavior? If you also believe in a God that punishes evildoers, do you think we're co-operating with God by treating our enemies this way, or that we'll get our just desserts for what we're doing when the time comes? In their eyes, we're the evildoers to their people.

Does it bottom line to "They don't believe in God the way I do. Therefore they are not made by God; not made in the image and likeness of God. So I can do to them what I pray they never do to me."

We gloss over the death toll from the other side every time we're in a violent conflict. Seeing the pictures we've been seeing recently has shown us our dark side, dramatically.

We're the only ones who can change it. If you feel its wrong, do something.

June 5, 2004

Potter books can be teaching tools of Christian faith

Do you remember the uproar a couple years ago when the first Harry Potter book came out? Some parents were extremely concerned about the imagery, and their children's souls and minds.

Other parents saw no threat and were thrilled that their kids had their noses in a book rather than their eyes stuck to the tube.

While adults can make decisions for themselves, a parent must gauge the effect material will make on their offspring and make choices for them.

The concerns have to do with the framework of the books, i.e. wizardry, magic, the occult. Would exposing a child to this type of material open a door to the antithesis of their Christian beliefs? Would allowing their child(ren) to participate in the phenomenon of Harry Potter give credence to what it "taught"?

Two Christian writers have books I've encountered recently on the subject. The first is, "What's a Christian To Do With Harry Potter?" by Connie Neal, and the other is "Looking for God in Harry Potter" by John Granger.

John Granger, who has written extensively about the Potter series, will be at the Silverdale Barnes & Noble on Friday June 11th at 7:00 pm, speaking and signing copies of his new book.

The word "occult" hits a raw nerve for many people, sending up a red flag of alarm. It conjures up memories of what they've been taught about good and evil, witches and warlocks. The word itself, however, is innocuous. It means "hidden" or "invisible."

It could be said, then, that many in the world find their purpose for living occult; they don't know why they're here. The air is occult unless there's something floating in it.

Many pray to God, "creator of all that is seen and unseen." Well, that's pretty spooky, don't you think? Growing up with that prayer, I thought of angels and black holes, not principalities and the effects of black magic.

The Potter books, we're told by these two writers, can be great teaching tools about the Christian faith and virtues in general. For example, Neal, in a movie discussion guide for parents, lists bravery, friendship, values, resisting temptation, and a host of other "teachable moments" that her book can provide. Due to space restrictions I can't go into detail on the good insight these authors provide, but do remember you'll have one in your midst next week.

For myself, the idea of spells and such causes wariness. Probably because I was taught at an early age that it calls on a power that isn't God, and that is not something you'd want to mess with. Yet I was taught at the same time that God is "the creator of all that is seen and unseen." How can this be? What does it mean? Theologians have been studying and commenting on this for eons and the responses can differ. Learned people can read the same scripture and come out with opposite beliefs.

Is your belief the only right one?

June 19, 2004

In words and actions, we should love God's creations

Once in a while I send out an email to my friends that I title, "A Reading From..." Most often its a reading from a favorite book or sermon I've experienced. The last one I sent (see below) was from Words To Live By by Eknath Easwaran. I often add commentary at the end, as I did here, because the reading elicited some deep reflection on my part that I wanted to share.

It's good to think.

In this book, Easwaran starts out with a quote from a well-known author then provides some reflection. He is one of my very favorite writers, and I am eternally grateful to friend Carmel Pennington for giving me this book.

It begins with this quote from F. M. Dostoevsky, "Love all that has been created by God, both the whole and every grain of sand. Love every leaf and every ray of light. Love the beasts and the birds, love the plants, love every separate fragment. If you love each separate fragment, you will understand the mystery of the whole resting in God."

"Most of us" writes Eswaran, "think of love as a one-to-one relationship, which is the limitation of love on the physical level. But there is no limit to our capacity to love. We can never be satisfied by loving just one person here, another there. Our need is to love completely, universally, without any reservations. In other words, to become love itself."

Recently I read that a flame-retardant chemical used most often in the production of televisions, a human-made toxin, was found in Arctic wildlife - in polar bears and sea gulls.

When will we get it through our heads that we don't live alone on this planet? That the breath that is exhaled in Nairobi is the air breathed in by a soul a continent away? Are we "making a living", making a profit at any cost? We are so consumed with our little corner of the earth that we forget our decisions, and the decisions of every other being, have an effect on everything else, no matter how minute - or enormous. Think - think - think - whether that quick trip down to the store can wait - and avoid polluting the air just a little bit.

Think - about the effect eliminating just one cigarette or cigar or pipe for a day would make if done by a few million people.

Think – about the incredible value of double-hulled tankers in everybody's oceans.

Are we, as consumers and stockholders, so small-minded, short-visioned and in need of instant gratification that we can't do the right thing for our great grand kids? Live your life consciously.

Think about the extended ramifications of your behavior and the effect it can have on not just other humans, but on plants, fish, and animals. We take them all into our bodies. What are we then taking into our bodies?

We are ALL responsible for the safety, health and well being of our Mother. And each other.

July 10, 2004

Filing the gap from Sunday to Monday

In the latest e-newsletter I received from the Yale Center for Faith and Culture was the listing of a summer course titled, "Ministering to Those Called to the Marketplace: Overcoming the Sunday – Monday Gap." I was intrigued by its description, which asked: "How do clergy minister more intentionally to the needs and possibilities of those in the business world? If one's work doesn't matter to the pastor, how can it matter to God?"

In light of recent corporate scandals this interested me. But on a closer level, I wondered about the employee who occupies a pew on Sunday, yet feels its OK to steal a pack of pencils from the company storeroom on Monday.

The following is a portion of my interview with Dr. David W. Miller, Exec. Dir. of the Center (www.yale.edu/faith) and instructor of the course.

"Sir, what is that gap? Is it a breach in the ethics between being in the pew on Sunday and the boardroom on Monday? Is it the difference between what we hope for ourselves, sitting in church on Sunday, and our actions the rest of the week?"

"The gap I'm referring to is where the Sunday worship experience – from prayers to sacraments to sermons – while often meaningful and well administered – bear little relationship to a person's Monday workplace or office reality. This often leads to living a bifurcated life where we compartmentalize our faith as a private matter relegated to Sunday, and where our Monday is no longer shaped by or informed by our faith teaching."

"I understand your course has to do with the pastor's side of this. What is it that you believe pastors are preaching up there?"

"Many pastors are simply not trained to think about the church as anything other than the center of one's faith life. The church should be a means to equip the followers of Jesus to live out faith-filled lives Monday through Saturday. Many pastors have a theology that spiritualizes faith and takes it out of the realm of the nitty gritty of life. Yet the Bible gives a consistent message that people of faith are meant to be salt and light in the world. The best advice one might give future clergy is 'it's not about Sunday!' That reframing makes a huge difference in how clergy preach, pray, lead worship and teach."

"If you had to summarize your goal for this course, what would you hope the soul sitting in the church would get from a pastor that took this course?"

"The realization that our daily work matters to God; indeed, it matters deeply. Not only what we do but how we do it. And that the Christian faith is a rich resource to help us discern what lines of work to go into, and how to carry ourselves once we're there. Work can be a holy calling."

Is there a disconnect in your life between what you believe on Sunday and do on Monday, no matter what faith you practice? If so, ask yourself why.

July 31, 2004

It's a slippery slope to incivility

We, as a country, have sunk to a new low in our political debate. Attacks and counterattacks, threats, name-calling, betrayals, and the language... While all these are, unfortunately, normal for a major election year, many newspaper columns across the nation, and every news program I've seen, agree it is particularly vicious now.

It doesn't matter whether you declare yourself Republican, Independent, Green Party or Democrat, liberal or conservative or something in between – civility is in short supply.

We are so polarized. If you're for this, you can't be for that. We seem to be intolerant of shades, discussion and debate.

I am as guilty as the next person. A few carefully chosen words have crossed my mind in evaluating the present landscape.

Religion plays a big part of the picture. And I'm not talking about the candidates trying to sway votes from churches. I'm talking about what you're thinking and saying; what's in your heart.

How do our responses to the challenges we're facing now fit in with our beliefs and ethics? Do you think Moses or Jesus or Buddha would use the vile language, or hold the attitudes and grudges, and yes, hatred, a lot of us do right now?

You may say there is no room for tolerance when the lives of so many are on the line; that there is misrepresentation and the deliberate distortion of facts. I have no doubt of that! But does that give you permission to violate the rules you choose to live by when you're not so emotionally charged?

It is something I face myself: how to follow my truth and work to promote the vision I hold without turning my back on the rules for living I believe in. Rules such as "treat others as I would like to be treated" and "love God with your whole heart, soul, mind and strength." To my way of thinking, I can't be thanking and praising God with a loving heart in one breath and tearing apart my brother or sister in the other. To do otherwise is incompatible with what I hold dearest. Disagree, yes. Work to change what I believe is wrong, yes. Vilification? No.

Most of us can be masters of rationalization and justification when we need to be. Does saying "He deserves it!" or "I'm just so angry!" allow you to shoot right past what you hold as right when it suits you?

Perhaps you don't believe this applies to you. But have you consciously thought about what you're thinking? Do you engage in conversations that support this meltdown in ethics? I know I have, and now I am working on more closely monitoring my thoughts and behavior. I don't want to be a part of what is breaking down our national values and goals, or my personal spiritual beliefs.

Every day we have the ability and freedom to choose our path. We can wholeheartedly disagree and enthusiastically work to change what we believe is wrong without compromising ourselves.

August 14, 2004

Forgiveness opens the door to a new life

At our recent International Forgiveness Day observance, Rev. Dr. Rodney Romney said, "The choice to forgive or to hold onto grievances is a conscious one. When we choose to hold onto our grievances, we fill our minds with pain, conflict and suffering. When we choose to forgive, we immediately feel lighter, for much of the pain and suffering caused by our grievances disappears. Also, we are then freer to pursue the work of bringing about a peaceful solution to the conflict..."

Twenty years ago I sought a divorce from my emotionally and mentally abusive husband. I had a four-year-old son. Financial support from him for this precious child was hard to come by. Probably like most divorced mothers, money was tight.

When the water pump went out on my station wagon, I blamed him because I had no funds to replace it. When it was cold in winter and we were bundled up in double socks and could see our breath in our apartment, I blamed him. When our son went to school year after year in recycled clothes and came home sad because he was teased yet again, I blamed him. I was working full time and couldn't pay much more than the rent and utilities. There wasn't much misery I didn't lay on his doorstep.

One bright summer day a couple years later – I remember this so distinctly because it was a turning point in my life – I was sitting on the couch crying about how he did me wrong, when I heard the words, "I forgive you" come out of my mouth. No one was more shocked than I. I convulsed in tears so hard I could barely breathe. It literally felt as if I was sobbing from my soul. "I forgive you," I said over and over.

The relief I felt was monumental; it's hard to put into words. But Rod is exactly right. It was like walking around in a blanket of muggy 100-degree heat, compared to the cool comfort of 68-degrees and rain. I felt as if a great burden had been lifted from me.

Days after going through this I realized I also had to forgive myself as well. I had expended so much time and energy in anxiety and fear that I could have spent being present to my son. Again I seized up crying on the couch feeling sorry for myself. I realized then that I had to say to myself what, with God's grace, I had been able to say about my mom – she did the best she could with what she had and what she knew.

Does feeling joyful weigh you down? No. Does carrying hatred or grudges lift your spirits? No. Do you need help in getting out from under that hot blanket? Ask your Creator for guidance and you'll be shown the way, if you want to see. Some folks have an investment in hanging on to pain. But we haven't got time for it.

August 28, 2004

Relationships are the building blocks of life

A friend of mine recently began a new job, which took him away from the people he'd worked and grown with for many years.

At the ceremony marking his departure and advancement, he stood before a large group of peers and well-wishers, and said what he would miss most was the relationships; the bonds that had been forged over years of interaction, respect and appreciation.

These words of his have stuck with me for weeks, and caused me to reflect on my relationships, and the ones we have as "humanity."

We are in relationship to everyone around us, such as our family, friends and co-workers, along with the driver in the car next to us on the road and the kid in the window at Wendy's. The caregiver who bathes us in the nursing home and the cop who helps us look for a lost child.

You and I have a relationship.

We are in relationship with everything around us. Consider the lilies, trees and pollen, vehicles and motor oil, health and pills, newspapers and ink, your bed, blanket, and breakfast. Where and how they are grown, who builds them or makes it, what the source of labor or product is touches you every moment of your life. We do not live in a vacuum.

Listening to the speeches these days, i.e., "If I'm elected I promise to..." always disturbs me because no one does it alone. You can have the grandest goals, but others can thwart them. Yet we have faith in this process; we have a relationship with it.

There is one relationship that acts as an umbrella over everything in your life. It is felt in your judgment for a baby sitter, the type of gasoline you buy, and the person you vote for; in what you eat, wear, think, read, feel and believe. And that is your relationship with your Creator.

There is no situation you could find yourself in that God is not. If you attend a house of worship, you do not leave your belief system at the door when you walk out. At least I hope you don't. Your belief in your deity and what it stands for should affect your ethics and morality throughout the channels of your life.

Perhaps you've known of folks who sit across from you week after week in church, only to find them written up in the papers for misappropriation of funds or child abuse. A definite disconnect from their belief system. Is this something your God would condone as loving and compassionate, fair and wise? As John C. Maxwell writes, "There is no such thing as business ethics."

Whether you like it or not, your life is your message. What does yours say about you? Can you see, and can others see, that your relationship with God is the ground of your being?

Congratulations to the people of Gig Harbor and their new Chief of Police Mike Davis. May they continue to forge a mutually beneficial relationship together.

September 11, 2004

Peace grows one person at a time

Today is certainly a day that will "live in infamy." It is the third anniversary of 9/11, a date burned into America's collective consciousness as the day we lost our innocence after being attacked by a small group of people on our soil.

They certainly believed in Gandhi's powerful message, "Be the change you want to see in the world." Look what they accomplished.

We went on the offensive, seeking out any one or organization that may have contributed to our devastation, in an attempt to defend ourselves in the future and make the perpetrators pay.

We reached the milestone earlier this week of losing 1000 of our sons and daughters to the war in Iraq.

This month also saw the tragedy in Russia with the loss of hundreds of souls in a school uprising caused primarily, we are told, by Chechnyans demanding an end to the killing of their people by the Russian military.

In the Sudan, reports The Detroit Free Press, over 30,000 have been killed and a million displaced. Many are children literally thrown into blazing fires in an effort to rid the land of those who would come to inherit it.

"The violence is an outgrowth of a civil war pitting black African rebels against the Arab militias fighting on behalf of the Sudanese government, which denies it controls them. The militias have waged a forced eviction campaign against villagers tribally linked to the rebels. The goal, in part, is to drive them away and use their farming lands as grazing areas for Arab herder communities," we read.

And then there is the Middle East, Bosnia, Afghanistan, North Korea...

Is there no peace to be found anywhere? Is it only possible if everybody agrees to abide by the same rules? The way things are now, if you can't defend yourself you end up like the Sudanese - victims to the will of those stronger than you. And then there is revenge.

Will we ever see the lions and the lambs of the world looking after each other? Religion has much to say about this; there are many differing views. I think the bottom line lies with what is in each individual's heart.

At the end of their service, the congregation of West Sound Unity in Bremerton sings, "Let there be peace on earth and let it begin with me."

Peace has to blossom into fruition in each soul. It's in the way you think, the way you approach life's situations, the way you do your politicking. It's in the language you use when you speak to yourself or others, the way you look at the homeless and those better off than yourself. If we each work to remove violence from our hearts and spirits, we will be the light we want to see in the world.

We must each be the change we want to see in the world.

In the words of a well-known ad, "Do you have it in you?"

September 25, 2004

Revealing a secret; finding support

I went to see my internist recently about the effects that long-term, high stress was having on me physically. Being a Type 2 diabetic of many years, I know it could have a profound affect on my health. Cortisol, the "fight, flight or freeze" hormone produced by stress, works against insulin. The notion that any of the shots I give myself daily might be in vain caused, well, more stress.

He said he wanted to put me on an anti-depressant, which affects cortisol. I took note of my strong negative reaction and said there had to be another way of dealing with this. I didn't want to take some medication that would affect my mind or my thinking. At the time I didn't consider the aspirin I take or the occasional marguerita with the girls.

I told him I was going to see a counselor, too, to see if I could change any behaviors. That's great, he said, but I still want you to take these.

Driving home, I asked myself where did this visceral feeling came from.

My mother. Life had been so hard for her that her doctor had put her on one of these, too, in her later years. I used to pick them up from the pharmacy for her. She wasn't the same person after a while. Her energy went flat and she became withdrawn. I attributed that to the drugs she was taking. Granted, this was in the '80's, I told myself, and formulations may have changed. But I didn't want that to happen to me. I didn't know what to do.

I stared at the prescription at home, praying, and asking for guidance. The thought occurred to me that I didn't have to tell anyone; no one had to know. But that didn't sit well with me. Was diabetes a personal weakness? Isn't this just another chemical imbalance? Yesssss, I grudgingly agreed. But there is no stigma to diabetes. For me it's a disease passed down in my family. Was I just worried, then, about what people would think if they knew? Wouldn't they think less of me, like I thought less of others? Ouch! I was biased and hadn't consciously known it. Yet here I was, face to face with it.

I've always believed that God graced humanity with intelligence to remedy the afflictions of life. The use of SSRI's (or anti-depressants) does not signify moral or emotional failure. In fact, I've come to the conclusion that it takes strength to help yourself, knowing that many may view you differently. I've sought counsel from several individuals I trust, only to hear them state they take them but can't tell anyone for fear of smudging their careers. And these folks were just fine. They weren't like my mom, and they trusted me enough to share their secret with me to help me find peace.

So now I share my secret with you. God can work in wondrous ways to make your life better. If you need help with the incredible stresses of life, see your doctor.

October 9, 2004

Religious debate is a good thing

These can be tough times for people of faith. Debates on the death penalty, stem cell research, abortion, and political connections with churches are heard on the airwaves, at the dinner table and around the water cooler. This is good.

The final outcome of your decision-making may depend on the core beliefs of your religion.

Lots of folks identify themselves as Christians. Yet the criteria can be quite different depending on the denomination you identify with from under that umbrella.

There are dozens of larger groups and within them are offshoots or branches. Just saying you're Lutheran, for example, doesn't say if you're with the Lutheran Church Missouri Synod (LCMS) or the Evangelical Lutheran Church in America (ELCA). They are not the same in their beliefs. Is one right and the other wrong because they don't agree on the same things? Because of a disagreement on a fundamental issue, is one "right" with God and the other not?

There are those, too, that believe both testaments in the Bible are literal. Those that believe there are a number of literary forms used. Those that believe Jesus to be a prophet only. Those that believe the book is alive and that the Holy Spirit inspires the souls of women and men through the ages on how to apply its teachings to the present day. Those that believe that God is male and those that don't.

So what are the core beliefs of Christianity? Is there a common denominator that crosses all dividing lines?

Again, different groups believe differently. Those that believe the Bible is the literal word of God have a different answer than those that believe it is inspired from age to age. And that in itself is a major one.

Then there are those called "Cafeteria Christians" - those that are criticized for not joining with one group or another, but taking those aspects from one or several groups that supports their spiritual journey. These are often referred to as the "unchurched." Because they do not fit neatly into one of the many boxes already established, they are often looked down upon by those inside the boxes. Yet those boxes were made by people like these, who are trying to find the best way to connect with their understanding of God.

Many people these days state that they are "spiritual but not religious." People I've spoken with who state this say they are "turned off" by the hierarchical structure of organized religion, or the "one size fits all" nature of a denomination's teachings. Often they have incorporated components of other faith traditions, or feel they have examined the teachings of their youth and are searching for their own path. They are, I believe, no less loved or in love with God than those that occupy a pew on Sundays and Wednesdays.

Perhaps the common denominator could be the journey with the Creator, and it takes in all of humanity's faith traditions, not just Christianity. We are souls on a mission, and all due the respect of each other.

October 30, 2004

Is the Golden Rule really attainable?

The scriptures of the Zoroastrian, Hindu, Islamic, Jewish, Christian and Bahai traditions (among others) all make reference to The Golden Rule, i.e. "Do to others as you would like done to you."

These are examples of the Ethic of Reciprocity which in broad terms states that every human being has value and is due respect, simply because they're alive.

Rev. Dr. Martin Luther King, Jr. is quoted as saying, "Man must evolve for all human conflict a method which rejects revenge, aggression and retaliation. The foundation of such a method is love."

Surely, over millennia, we have, as humanity, been moving toward this goal. But does this kind of understanding and unconditional "agape" love come from our own souls? Can mere mortals aspire to such greatness of spirit?

Rabbi Israel Baal Shem Tov traveled Eastern Europe in the 18th century, igniting an exuberant form of Judaism known as Chasidism. He wrote, "There are some who seek God, but they believe that the Divine is very far away, surrounded by many high walls.

And when they fail in their search they say, 'I sought him but I found him not' (Song of Songs 3:1).

Had they been wise, however, they would have known that 'there is no place empty of God' (Tikkuney Zohar 57:91b). You can find God in everything! You can find God everywhere!

Understand this: when you discover Divinity in any facet of reality and bind your consciousness to that portion of God, you are binding yourself to the All in all."

There are those who say it is naive to believe The Golden Rule is realistic; something that can be lived out. It's a nice thought, yes, but in the real world there are people that hijack kids on their way to school, or hate Americans, or steal our identities. How do you reconcile your feelings on this?

Who does this rule apply to? Does it have a limit? Is it one of those "commands" that is negotiable, depending on the circumstances? The different degrees it is taken to depend on the understanding or acceptance of what it calls forth from you.

When asked what the greatest law was, the Bible says Jesus' reply was, "Love God with all your heart, all your soul, all your mind, and all your strength. The second is similar: love your neighbor as yourself."

These are inextricably tied with The Golden Rule.

Here we see that this is the desire of humanity, and because many believe we are made in the image and likeness of our Creator, bound to the All by a love and attachment we still don't fully understand, we, as individual souls, have the ability to make the choice and work to make it real.

My mom had a saying: "It's easy to love when it's easy; anybody can do that. When it's hard to love someone and you do, it's of God."

Change the color of the skin or hair, the shape of the nose or chin; the dialect and customs. We are all just humanity on this earth together.

November 13, 2004

Strip away standard perceptions of God

I tore my house apart last week looking for my spare color ink cartridge. It wasn't where it should have been. After checking out my office area I moved to the kitchen; had I left it in a bag maybe? Back to the office/bedroom, I looked on the ironing board, under the bed, in a box on the worktable. Zippo. I sat on my chair in front of the computer, wondering where else it could possible be when... there it was sitting on top of my disc box. It was there, hidden in plain sight, the whole time. What I'd been looking for was the familiar box – not the cartridge itself.

In "The Ladder", a book of modern day parables by Edward Hays, he tells the story of a young man who is on his way to spend a few days in a spiritual retreat. The goal, he says, is to "encounter God." Remarking on the immenseness of his suitcase, his teacher says he may have difficulty being naked before God.

"If you want not only the guest master but also God to meet you at the front gate, strip yourself of your agenda for your retreat. Unpack your books, tapes, and even your Bible. Strip yourself of your habitual ways of how you see, feel and think about yourself, how you think about your daily world and most of all, how you think about God. Unpack as well your attachments and preconceptions. Take nothing on retreat except the naked you, the old original you. If you can go on retreat in this way – completely naked – be assured that you will encounter God on the mountain."

There have been a few times in my life when I truly thought I'd be struck down by lightening for the thoughts that had entered my mind. The things we are taught to believe and do by our particular faith can be hard to dislodge. When a new perception gets a foothold in your thinking, and it's not along the lines you were taught, fear can rear its head and you proceed cautiously, if not disregarding it altogether.

We know, though, don't we, that if someone were to question the dogma of their faith to move to ours, well, they would just be doing what's right. Right?

If, however, you have come to know the still, small voice of your creator, and you trust it, and it's moving you off the highway, you know you must honor it no matter what other's think of you. It's the only way you find peace.

It can be very difficult to strip yourself of the "habitual ways" you think about God. Often, all we have to do is suspend judgment on someone in order to increase the light, to see God's presence from another perspective. God can be hiding in plain sight, just in a different wrapper. God has much more to reveal to us, if only we have eyes to see and ears to hear.

November 27, 2004

In need of a good hug

There are times, even as old as I am, when what I want most is to be held by someone older and bigger than me. Someone who will just let me hang on for a few minutes, for dear life. Cry if I need to. Sing if I need to. Give me that sense of protection from the world I never had as a child. I don't ever remember a time when I received that. It may be an ache that I die with.

My dad passing away when I was a tot, and two short-lived marriages that hindsight revealed were not made in heaven, never afforded me this gift. I've gotten by, of course. I participate in a lot of hugs with friends. But this is a particular type of connection. Lots of folks never receive it.

It's times like this, when we get all mushy during the holidays and our expectations for family unity are so high, that the sense of loss is most acute.

A couple weeks back I was watching a favorite show, "Joan of Arcadia", when Joan was in a hospital hallway wailing to God (played by Kathryn Joosten, Mrs. Landingham of "The West Wing") about the death of a friend. Inconsolable, Joan is gathered up into the arms of God. Oh, how I've longed all my life for that. I caught my breath and absolutely understood the comfort that can only be found in knowing that you are known, understood, loved deeply and unconditionally.

Years ago I'd yell at and for God, crying out in misery, "Where are you? Why aren't you here in a body to hold me and help me through this? You said you'd take care of me. Where are you?"

We are the embodied extension of our faith in the divine. We are the ears that listen to the heartbreak, the hearts that act from compassion, the arms that hold and console.

Often we are hostages to our memories. We carry weight that has nothing to do with an extra piece of Aunt Vivian's pecan pie. It's the weight of unforgiveness. The weight of not letting bygones be bygones. The weight of carrying sadness over the loss of a loved one, too soon gone. Some things can be changed, others can't. But we can always choose mercy for others and ourselves.

Emotions run high this time of year for most folks. There are always stories that emerge about a dreaded confrontation with a family member, or someone mourning the loss of a beloved. You have the power to effect a change in these lives.

If it's you carrying a grudge, consider forgiveness. If you know of someone who is now alone, consider opening your door and heart to them. Reach out and across any anger or pain and build a bridge to healing. You can do it. God can help.

Give the benefit of the doubt. We are all just souls at our centers, trying to make our way in a troubled world.

2005

January 8, 2005

Slow down, make an impact

I began writing this column for The Sun in January of 1999; this begins my sixth year.

During the course of these years, I have chatted with folks in stores, or corresponded with many of you through cards, letters or emails. And not just locally. When the column was picked up by Scripps Howard News Service a couple years ago, I began hearing from folks across the U.S. I'll never forget the atheist gentleman from Texas who wrote me. At one point I asked him why he was reading a spirituality column and contacting me if he held such a belief. His response was, "You never know what might change my mind."

You never know when what you say or do may influence someone's relationship with their Creator. Especially if you're known in your community for encouraging such behavior.

Recently I was in a hurry and was abrupt with a bank teller in a drive-through window. I hadn't had to go through the process before of coming in to the building and providing an inked thumbprint on a holiday check I was trying to cash and send to my son. They asked for two pieces of picture ID. I only had my driver's license and I pulled out every piece of ID in my wallet for them to see. I'm thinking, "This is ridiculous!" and a senior bank employee came over to assist. She looked at my license, then at my face. "I recognize her from her picture in the paper. Go ahead and cash it."

I was mortified; beyond embarrassed. I apologized for my attitude, but there was no excuse. I realized I had failed to walk my talk. I was no representative of the loving kindness I write about. I had blown a chance to be a witness to my beliefs, and abysmally so. I can only hope to learn from this, and to be forgiven.

Life is pretty busy for most folks. I don't think we consciously go through our days thinking we're a representative of our beliefs, tradition, faith or denomination, but we are.

My son Gabriel has a favorite quote from St. Francis, "Preach the Gospel at all times, and if necessary, use words." That could apply to anyone of any faith, with a little modification. Actions speak louder than words. "They'll know that we're (insert your choice: Christian/Bahai/Muslim, etc.) by our love."

Friend Mike said something a couple months ago that I wrote about then, and it has taken on even more importance recently. He said, and I paraphrase, "It's all about our relationships." Our relationships with our immediate neighbors, and as we're seeing now, our neighbors overseas as well. "They'll know we're good neighbors by our love."

Try being more conscious about whether your behavior matches your beliefs, and your words. You never know who may be watching to see the reality of your nature. Credibility comes when they go hand in hand. As my Texan friend wrote, "You never know what might change my mind."

January 22, 2005

Reading to a stronger faith

Here is my fifth annual list of recommended reading for the new year.

Because this column is nonsectarian, i.e. not affiliated with or restricted to a particular religious group, and works to promote all souls spiritual pursuits, the materials listed below reflect this goal. Take what suits you, supports your vision, and maybe inspires you to find out what your brothers and sisters believe, too.

Across the world's religions, there is more that unites us than divides us. While there are, of course, undeniable core faith issues that create a specific identity, we can operate strongly from within those structures to promote common denominators. Huston Smith's "The World's Religions: Our Great Wisdom Traditions" does an excellent job of presenting their history and fundamental beliefs. In our age, when we now realize that a breath exhaled on one continent impacts lives on another, and wars rage around the world because of religious disagreements, ignorance is not bliss. No one is asking or recommending that you change your faith; only that you understand that the way to permanent peace in our relationships with each other and across our earth may be in understanding where others are coming from; what their motivation is, and seeing if there isn't some way to make them dovetail.

Other worthy books along this line are "A History of God: The 4,000-Year Quest of Judaism, Christianity and Islam" by Karen Armstrong, "When Faiths Collide" by Martin Marty, and "The Mystic Heart: Discovering a Universal Spirituality in the World's Religions" by Wayne Teasdale.

Books I'm reading right now are "Illuminated Life: Monastic Wisdom for Seekers of Light" by Joan Chittister, "The Holy Longing: The Hidden Power of Spiritual Yearning" by Connie Zweig, "The Fabric of the Cosmos: Space, Time, and the Texture of Reality" by Brian Greene, and "Stillness Speaks" by Eckhart Tolle.

On my "to read" list are "When Jesus Came to Harvard: Making Moral Choices Today" by Harvey Cox, "Healing Through the Dark Emotions: The Wisdom of Grief, Fear, and Despair" by Miriam Greenspan, "Seeing God – Ten Life Changing Lessons of the Kabbalah" by David Aaron, "The Hidden Messages in Water" by Masaru Emoto, and "The Wisdom of Forgiveness" by H.H. Dalai Lama.

Reading material comes out of my grocery budget because I feel I'm feeding my body, soul and spirit. Please make reading a priority in your life and your family's. In periodicals, I subscribe to "Spirituality and Health", "Science and Theology News", "Discovery", "Science and Spirit", and "Sacred Journey." If I had more money, there's a few more I'd get.

Perennial favorites include, "Wilderness Spirituality" by Rev. Dr. Rodney Romney, and "St. George and the Dragon" by Edward Hays.

There is no subject that's a part of our existence that God doesn't relate to. You and God are inseparable, whether you acknowledge it on a daily basis or not. Learning about another's faith can make you stronger in yours; in fact, that is the goal of every interfaith council I've known.

February 5, 2005

How is values a buzzword?

The issue of values played a large part in our recent elections. Political parties threw that word around like dropping it would get them a good table at a classy restaurant. They both said that was what they stood for, supported, and would work to promote.

But are all values created equal?

My brother, who served in Vietnam in the Marines, called recently to ask that question.

"Let me get this straight," he said. "We can invade a country that has done nothing to us, and in the name of bringing them democracy, freedom, and our better way of life, wipe out an estimated 20,000 Iraqi people, among them pregnant women so that's two right there, and children, declare it moral, and then work against abortion in this country? It doesn't add up. Either life is sacred across the board or it isn't.

You know what they say, I told him. The good of the many outweighs the good of the individual.

"But we all stand up and beat people over the head with our idea of 'high moral values' and say absolutely nothing about only God knows how many families we took out. We can kill pregnant women in war and that's OK, and then we have the nerve to say as a government that we oppose abortion? What kind of value is that?"

As individuals and as a nation we often have conflicting values. When we can't or don't want to face the contradictions in ourselves, we put blinders on and act like everything's fine. Others can point it out to us but we're stubborn. Examining the situation, the schizophrenic break in our moral value system, would cause a tsunami-like cascade of change in our lives as individuals and a nation. If we were to acknowledge that the "collateral damage" of war, i.e. the unintended yet unavoidable loss of innocent lives was wrong, intolerable, and violated our moral values... we couldn't live with ourselves. It would absolutely change everything about us as a country.

"What's amazing to me," he continued, "is that we hold up God as our compass, our guide. We go to war because of the values we say God expects us to live up to. How crazy is that? Aren't we practicing 'moral relativism'? What kind of God says its OK to send young kids fresh out of high school into a war zone where they're faced literally with blood and guts and death; where they will have to shoot a bullet that they see enters a person and kills them? I know what its like to come back after living through that. It's wrong, Sal. It's just wrong."

We want peace. Our kids of whatever age put themselves in harm's way to protect us from others who may also want peace, but on their terms like we do ours. So we play a devastating chess game on planet Earth all the time, struggling with our beliefs, our values, and in war, absolutely nobody wins.

March 5, 2005

Religion, spirituality: which fits best?

There is a difference between spirituality and religion.

How do you define the two terms?

I wish those who prefer one way of being to the other could respect each other's choices and not dismiss either way as having less value than the other.

In "The God Gene – How Faith is Hardwired Into Our Genes," author Dean Hamer says, "Spirituality is intensely personal; religion is institutional."

You could view spirituality as a person's relationship with their creator, universe, and others. Your religion most often reflects your belief in a particular leader and their teachings. You can choose to live out your spirituality as a Methodist, Mormon, or Muslim, for example.

In "Spirituality for Dummies" by Sharon Janis, she states that spirituality is "the mystical face of religion." It is our connection to all that is seen and unseen.
You could participate in a faith community and not be spiritual – enjoying the structure of law more than the spirit and love it offers.

"Spirituality is the wellspring of divinity," she says, "that pulsates, dances, and flows   as the essence of every soul. It relates more to your personal search, to finding greater meaning and purpose in your existence." Many choose to do this inside the structure of a religious organization.

She continues, "Religion is most often used to describe an organized group or culture that has generally been sparked by the fire of a spiritual or divine soul. Religion usually acts with a mission and intention of presenting specific teachings and doctrines, while nurturing and propagating a particular way of life."

Do you agree?

Frederic Lenoir, editor of the French magazine "World of Religion" wrote, "The need for meaning affects the secularized and de-ideologized West most of all. Ultra-modern individuals mistrust religious institutions and they no longer believe in the radiant tomorrow promised by science and politics; they are still confronted, though, by the big questions about origins, suffering and death."

Being part of a faith community can help you find answers to those questions. It can give you, as Dr. Phil puts it, "a safe place to fall" when the trials of life are overwhelming, and be a place for you to use your talents and gifts to benefit others.

Whether Jewish, Christian, Muslim, or any one of the other hundreds of religions of humanity, or if you express your spirituality with meditation and prayer, working with a food bank, or admiring the beauty of a bearded iris, it's all about strengthening our relationship with, and love of, our creator – however we perceive it.

Explore and do what you feel is right in order to develop this life giving and sustaining bond.

April 2, 2005

Easier said than lived in today's world

Last Sunday was Easter. The greatest holy day for most Christians, it marks the resurrection of Jesus of Nazareth, who is now called "the Christ" (in Greek, Christos, or Anointed One.)

For those not Christian, there are benefits to understanding many of the underlying meanings of this yearly observance.

It can provide an opportunity to engage in personal transformation. Frequently that is aided by observing the 40-day period that precedes Easter called the season of Lent, which is a time of introspection and reflection.

One of the very best trainings I received growing up Roman Catholic was the examination of conscience. While important all year long, it took on special emphasis during Lent. The goal was to look for ways you could more closely emulate the life of Jesus.

Jesus routinely went apart from his disciples and friends to pray, or to more closely connect with the divine. There, he found strength. For us, it can be difficult to tap into the understanding of what is of the highest and best good for others and ourselves when we often have conflicting interpretations of scripture and competing priorities.

We still find ways to justify behavior that Jesus would never have approved of, according to what we read of his life in the Bible and the dozens of gospels and other writings that didn't make it in to that book.

We as a people in these United States don't condone torture, for example, but we approve representatives of us sending people off to countries that don't have a problem with it. We tell ourselves it's a "necessary evil" to save more people from harm. This is Christian behavior? Is this what Jesus would have done?

If we truly disapproved of this action, we'd raise a stink over it. But we don't. It fades from view and importance; we tacitly approve by our non-action.

We have problems now that 1st century souls never thought of, but many remain the same. We still cheat on our tax returns and spouses. We still struggle with morals, ethics, and war.

What Christians were left with when Jesus left Earth was big picture guidance. In order to translate the guidance from the big screen to our individual TV's, so to speak, many seek out a converter, or leader, to interpret the big screen message and guide them. Some simply go by what they believe is personal guidance from God to their spirit. All have merit, yet all guidance received is taken in through our own filters of beliefs, experiences, and training. That is why you can have two people who call themselves Christians be on totally opposite sides of an issue.

Is there a bottom line, though, a line in the sand that requires no interpretation?

"Rabbi," we read in Matthew, "of all of the commandments, which is the most important?"

Jesus replied, "To love God with your whole heart, soul, and mind. And the second is like it: love your neighbor as yourself."

Easier said than done.

April 16, 2005

John Paul was model for learning from others

Pope John Paul II will be remembered for many years to come, for many reasons.

In a life so visible to others, he clearly "walked his talk." His attempt to follow the example in living of Jesus of Nazareth was known to the world.

As with Jesus, his decisions weren't always popular. But you knew why he made them, even if you disagreed. This is one of the reasons why so many people of different cultures and religions respected him.

In the weeks that have followed his passing, much has been made of his work promoting interfaith dialogue, and his efforts to mend the fabric of world peace, ripped and threadbare in spots. In his travels, John Paul II sought to heal divisions by understanding and respecting other faith journeys.

Clearly, his adherence to his religion was not threatened by his interaction with those of other faiths. Much was made at the time when he held the Koran, the sacred scriptures of the Muslims, and kissed it. Yet Pope John Paul II knew that most of the terror in our world today is caused by a religious "us and them" mentality that does not seek to find our similarities, but emphasize our differences.

It was touching to see all the souls that spent great sums of money and traveled long distances to pay their respects to Pope John Paul II. The harder part, possibly, would be to follow his example in this area.

Growing up Roman Catholic in the '60's, I had to seek permission from my pastor to attend a friend's baptism in a Baptist church. How things have changed. And how they remain the same. In my interfaith work these days, I see fear in the eyes and behavior of many pastors. They set the tone and direction of their congregations, and they either covertly or overtly discourage interfaith contact. They don't want the members of their flock to be exposed to any faith other than their own because they might be seduced away and lose their salvation; they might be led astray by a particular teaching; they might question what they've always believed to be true.

Yet faith by its very nature is a belief in something unseen. Much like Indiana Jones, we step out on faith into the world, trusting in the guidance we receive from our creator and other human beings. Sometimes it takes us places we haven't been before, and sometimes it tells us to stay the course.

The interfaith groups I've worked with seek to promote peace through understanding world religions. Their goal isn't to take someone away from their faith, but to bridge this chasm of information with education. And we know that most of the conflicts in the world have at their source a lack of tolerance for other faith systems.

"Be not afraid."

May 7, 2005

You are wonderful for what you bring to the table

Martin Buber, in his book "I and Thou" wrote, "That you need God more than anything, you know at all times in your heart. But don't you know also that God needs you? You need God in order to be, and God needs you - for that which is the meaning of your life."

Reflecting on the above, Brother Wayne Teasdale writes in "The Mystic Hours", "Many who have chosen the spiritual path understand our need for the Divine, but few realize that God needs us."

He continues, "Each one of us here in this world, and all beings in every other world, universe, or more subtle realm, is required for God to be all in all. We all lean on God for our existence and for the continuity of being after this life, but we are all aspects of God's fuller reality and all that creation contains everywhere and at every time.

It is essential that each one of us achieves our potential for holiness, wisdom, and love in our present existence, for in this way, we contribute to the Absolute's perfection in relation to created or emanated being, reality, and manifestation."

It is essential that we be all we can be, whatever that may be. Those who transgress - ourselves included - are learning fodder, if you will, for others. For whatever you bring to the table, you're supposed to be here, now.

All things, not some things, work together for good for those who love God, yes? That is because you have eyes that see and ears that hear the underlying truth.

We are all familiar with the plight of Terri Schiavo and her families.

Whatever your position on the feeding tube, the entire situation caused us to ponder the value of life and contemplate abortion, death penalty, and euthanasia issues. While this situation was absolutely tragic, your thoughtful reflection on this assisted in your growth, as does every event and person in your life.

Even if you are a victim in a tragedy, and we all have been at one time, there is meaning. There is the possibility for growth in holiness and wisdom for all souls when seen in the light of God's love and devotion to you.

When we all fully understand that we have purpose and play a very real part in the existence of our Creator just by being who and what we are now... no one could possibly have low self-esteem.

There are those who may never in any way live what we would call a redeemed life, yet their existence is crucial to our spiritual development.

Yes, its painful to experience tragedy in any form, but from the trials of our life and others can come great growth in compassion, forgiveness, empathy and love.

You are wonderful beyond measure for what you bring to the table of life, imperfections and all. Never doubt that your value extends far beyond what you can imagine.

June 11, 2005

Wash window of your heart

Pushing back the sliding glass half panel on my kitchen window to let in clean, rain scrubbed air, I realized I was now looking through two glass panels that made the leafy green trees outside look dusty and indistinct.

If I didn't know any better, I would assume that was how things really were. Both views are real; both reflect reality. And truly, even if I was outside looking at these beautiful behemoths, could I say that I am seeing them as they really are?

We see the surface of everything; the visible sign of an inward process.

Trees, like humans, stars, and bicycle tires, have a common denominator to their existence, and that is the realm of quantum mechanics.

Every thing, literally, has atoms consisting of some combination of electrons, neutrons, and protons. So even though we're looking at the tree we're only "seeing" part of what makes it – it.

You've heard the story about the four people, each on a corner, witnessing an accident. Seeing the same event from four different angles, they have four different perceptions. Add to that mix that one person was five years of age, one was a young man 7' 2" in height, one elderly woman with cataracts stood in the shadow, and the fourth was an attorney specializing in personal injury.

What they saw was their reality; the same thing seen in very different ways because education, culture, life experience, and physical and mental abilities differ for every individual.

Just because someone believes something different than you do doesn't make them wrong.

We have faith – not only because of what we've seen, but also because of what we know in our spirits and souls to be true.

We are so frequently critical of what others believe. How many sons and daughters would have been spared for hundreds and hundreds of years if we hadn't needed to force our religious beliefs on others, whatever nation or people we were.

Preconceived notions, appearances, and assumptions are the dirty windows of our lives, keeping us from seeing what the heart of the matter truly is.

I know when I hear the words "politician" or "used car salesman", certain values come to mind that may not be valid with an individual, yet I've cast them all in a certain light.

Mother Teresa saw through the appearances of circumstance to the soul beneath, saying we are all Christ in our "distressing disguises." And they aren't just sickness, homelessness or poverty. They include sarcasm, fear, wealth and shallowness. I have no trouble seeing Christ in the struggle of an unemployed mother, but I sometimes struggle with seeing Christ in the over-indulged, pampered lifestyle of the rich and famous. Knowing in my heart, too, I wouldn't mind it for a week – at least.

Take some time to look beneath the surface of life. Understand that your reality isn't the only "right" one, and wash the windows of your heart. Even if you can't put yourself in their shoes, bless them anyway.

July 16, 2005

Real time pictures make suffering hard to ignore

We'd become comfortably numb.

If the world didn't know before about the plight of the people in Africa, they know now.

It is estimated that a billion of the planet's inhabitants either watched on television, over the Internet, or in person, the Live 8 concerts on July 2nd.

All the effort by hundreds of humanitarians to create these concerts around the globe was for one purpose: to make poverty history in Africa, where a child dies every three seconds due to malnutrition and disease, and where half the population is 16 or under because their parents have already died.

Fifty years or so ago, television was new. In just a few generations we've gone from the cathode ray tube to the global understanding of how one nation's behavior can affect all others, instantly.

Fifty years ago there was no real-time pictures from Darfur to Seattle. No watching David Bloom riding in the Iraqi desert at 3 a.m. our time to compensate for time zone changes.

When we, in the near future, reach the point where almost everyone on the planet can actually see the effects of their decisions on others as they happen, we will unequivocally understand that we are one people, one species among millions on this earth, with an awareness of our environment we can barely grasp now.

We are no longer comfortably numb, safe in our cocoon of unknowing. We can no longer claim innocence of the violence that is perpetrated on the unprotected. We know too much. Rapid-fire communication shrunk the world.

For the first time perhaps, youth heard that it is their responsibility, their privilege, to care for those suffering outside their line of sight. They heard how their choices, made in their hometowns, could affect a child in Zimbabwe.

And did you see all those gray heads in the crowds? We, too, so caught up in re-financing the house to pay down the cards, and figuring out where we want to spend next year's vacation, came away knowing we must make new priorities in our lives.

"We are not alone" is a line we use when referring to aliens from outer space. But we need to rethink it. Take care of those in our communities, yes, but those with more can do more. Those with excess can adopt a child through Save the Children or send a quarterly check with a bunch of zero's to Mercy Corp, Heifer, or World Vision.

You and I and our offspring will probably never have the wealth of a Gates or a Winfrey, but we can mobilize ourselves and others to help our brothers and sisters on this one earth.

Even if we don't do it out of the goodness of our hearts, but do it because it will make the planet more secure politically and financially, we must do it. We must take care of each other, wherever we are. We are interconnected, all from the one Source.

August 6, 2005

Forgiving is divine, but forgetting is something else

My mom taught me early on that "forgive and forget" went together like Rachmaninoff and joy. I found out later in life that wasn't true.

To forgive is good, a necessity. It heals your body, soul, mind and spirit. Forgetting is optional and should only be done when failing to remember would put you or another at risk for harm of any kind. To do otherwise invites victimization and you don't want to go there.

Fearful that her little daughters would face the same horrors of abuse she did as a child, mom would move us if she even thought she saw her brothers or uncles. We would leave our apartment in the middle of the night with one suitcase each and head to the bus station. There, she would put all the money she had on the counter and get us tickets to the farthest place the funds would take us. We would end up camped out outside the doors of the first church she found at the new destination. The sacrifices and hardship she went through to protect us, I can only imagine. She loved us very much. We stopped running when we were of an age that we could protect ourselves, and each other.

Eventually she understood that God may forget someone's transgressions – that was between them and their Maker - but it was her duty to protect her kids.

She learned that she could forgive them for what they did, but to forget would be devastating.

You may wonder, "How do I know I've truly forgiven someone? What does it look and feel like?" The best response I've heard, and I've found it to be true in my life, is that you know you've forgiven someone when they have safe passage through your mind. That is, you can think of the person or the event and you don't have a five-alarm response in your body.

To forgive doesn't mean you condone or approve of what happened. It doesn't mean that you don't seek justice. It does mean that you choose to release yourself from the emotional roller coaster that negatively impacts your whole being.

Think about how you feel physically when you are experiencing anger, fear, re-sentment, grief, or sadness - all factors of unforgiveness. Your body pumps chemicals into your system that research has shown, over time, can erode your immune system, impact your heart and blood pressure, and actually cause you to gain weight.

Everett L. Worthington, Jr., one of the world's pre-eminent researchers on forgive-ness says, in an article titled, "The Science of Forgiveness" (Fall 2004 issue of "Greater Good" magazine), that forgiveness is something that people can learn to do.

The person who hurt you may never know you did it; you're doing it for you, not for them. It can give you your life back, and give you back to your family and com-munity. We need you.

Forgiveness heals!

August 20, 2005

Living resurrection an everyday thing

One of the greatest aches of my life growing up was Easter. We spent so much time on the Via Crusis (Way of the Cross) and the Via Dolorosa (Way of Sorrow) but when it came to the resurrection, we gave it short shrift. The heavy emphasis was always on the Stations of the Cross. But it seemed to me that Easter and it's potential never reached the same status. We pretty much went back to business as usual after the egg hunt, Mass, and the bunny was returned to the store.

We were to focus on our sinful nature, i.e. "Father, I am not worthy to receive you..." even in light of the joy of Christ's return. Be happy but not too happy, was what I got, sitting in my pew on Sunday and in catechism class. Always remember you're a sinner, and you'll never be anything but a sinner.

OK.

Thumbing through my new issue of Sacred Journey recently, I spotted an article titled, "Stations of the Light" by Mary Ford-Grabowsky. My eyes filled with tears and I caught my breath. Here was the Via Lucis, the Stations of the Light or Resurrection. I'd never heard of them before. I'd wanted them forever.

There are 14 stations that take you from the resurrection to Pentecost, consisting of a Bible passage, a time of silence, a brief prayer, and then an Easter hymn.

It's the missing link.

It helps us see what new creatures we could be if we more fully lived the Easter message. This is of value for anyone looking to deepen their spirituality and quality of life.

The Archdiocese of Detroit on its Web site has a page devoted to the Via Lucis. It says that the official Vatican prayer book for the Jubilee Year 2000, Pilgrim Prayers, includes this devotion and states, "The Via Crusis reminds us that we are called to be crucifers. We take up the cross with the Risen Lord who teaches us and accompanies us through the challenges of daily life. The Via Lucis, a contemporary rediscovery of an ancient devotion, highlights the continuing presence of the Risen Lord, as we recognize His guidance and leadership through the events of our living. Walking the Via Lucis makes us lucifers, light bearers in a darkened world. This insight gives a whole new positive meaning to the name 'Lucifer' that was limited previously only to Catholic literary traditions' link with the name of the leader of the fallen angels."

Why bring this up when it isn't Easter? Because living the resurrection is an every day thing. Because along with bowing our heads in recognition of what we are, we can turn our faces up to the light, in recognition of what we are.

We are truly called to be bearers of the Light, understanding that Jesus has no body, now, but ours, to dry tears and bind wounds; praise good effort and speak for the poor; bring light into darkness.

August 27, 2005

On being liberal, conservative in light of the Bible

Growing up in the Roman Catholic tradition, I was taught that the Bible was "alive"; that it was a living document to be used by all ages for all ages. That the Holy Spirit moved souls then as now to interpret words written by human beings under inspiration of God thousands of years ago. That, if there was ever any question about what was the right overall view of anything we'd ever come up with, it would have to agree with what Jesus stated were the greatest laws: "Love God with your whole heart, soul, mind and strength, and your neighbor as yourself." That would be the litmus test for any Biblical interpretation.

That could be why slavery, permissible in the Bible in a letter from Peter and elsewhere, is not now. It does not support the greatest laws. It also shows that not every single word accepted by the Church Fathers for inclusion in the Canon supported what many believe to be God's "instructions."

Human beings are still being inspired by God, in no less a way than they have been since the dawn of humanity.

It seems the labels "liberal" and "conservative" have also been around for about as long. You can be one or the other in almost any subject you can name, religion and politics being primary among them.

The Rabbi Michael Lerner, author and editor of Tikkun (www.tikkun.org), a magazine of the interfaith movement, has spearheaded the creation of the Network of Spiritual Progressives whose goal is to "counter the religious right." Also, it focuses on what is perceived as a lack of both right and left, and that is community discussion on "values such as compassion, generosity, and helping the poor."

In an article in the Sacramento Bee, he states that, "The right doesn't think we can unify, and the left doesn't even want to talk about religion. A lot of them dismiss it." He states that after the 2004 elections, it became clear to him that exit polls showed "that many voters cast ballots based on religious beliefs and ethics, issues they felt were being addressed by Republicans and ignored by Democrats."

He's working to change that.

On July 20, over 1200 people gathered at a three-day, sold-out convention in Berkeley, CA called the "Reviving the American Spiritual Left - Tikkun Conference on Spiritual Activism." A second is scheduled in Washington, D.C., February 10-13, 2006.

Different religions, and the denominations within them (why have denominations unless you wish to promote a different aspect or belief from the parent religion?), believe God exists and functions in a multitude of different ways. Many believe their way of understanding the Source of All is the only true, viable one; the only one that will get you to heaven.

Others don't.

September 24, 2005

What about the soul?

Former President Bill Clinton said during an interview last Sunday, that Hurricane "Katrina is going to force us to go back and think about three things. What are our obligations to the poor, there, and in America? What is the role of government? And who's going to pay for it?"

There are those who have used Mark 14:7, "The poor you will always have with you, and you can help them any time you want", as a doorway to put off or do nothing for those struggling with less. We are not seeing anything of that nature in our community.

Day after day we're reading stories, seeing on television, and hearing of the heroism that bubbles up from us when we see another in need. Is there anyone who has not cried in anguish with the child who lost her mama, the frantic husband who couldn't find his beloved wife, the woman whose parent perished in a nursing home? It is our God given nature, I believe, to identify with broken hearts and spirits and try to help heal them. In this way, we are co-creators with the Creator of all that is seen and unseen.

Is there anyone among us who has not been able to identify in some way with the souls that have lost so much?

We are one. There is no us and them. We are one family, the family of humanity and it crosses every man-made boundary we've made in order to create tidy little boxes to define and separate ourselves from one another for a variety of purposes. Our community is pulling together its considerable resources in many ways to assist these folks rebuild their lives and develop new relationships.

Everything from car washes to spaghetti feeds; from collecting hygiene products to school supplies – we're doing whatever we can at every level to help relieve the suffering.

We're doing so much for the body – housing, health care, employment. What about their spiritual needs?

Mental health professionals are everywhere, helping them understand that their inability to string two thoughts together is normal under these circumstances. That feeling numb comes with overwhelming stress. That it will take time to make a new "normal".

Kitsap County is preparing for the possibility that many families from the Gulf Coast will move up here to join our community, and churches are mobilizing to meet not only the physical but the spiritual needs of our extended family.

One Church, One Family is working hard to prepare the way by connecting resources. Host families from these churches will provide, not just temporary shelter until the evacuees are situated, but the love, comfort, care and prayer they need. They, along with many others, will be Jesus' heart and hands because he has no hands, now, but yours, to extend compassion and action.

If you are a pastor and would be interested in participating with this group in some way, please contact Pastor Eric Glomstad from Sylvan Way Baptist Church, at (360) 373-5025.

October 22, 2005

Natural disasters not a message from above

There are those who believe that the devastation caused by Hurricane Katrina was God's smite upon Gulf Coast inhabitants. In other words, they (the unborn, pastors, and church-going moms and dads among them) were punished for their less than godly lifestyle. And we're not talking about just a couple strip clubs, oh no. If that were true Seattle would be next. Or maybe Gorst. No, we're talking big time bad stuff. Gambling (does bingo count?), drinking to excess, and unapproved sexual activity.

Perhaps when the Big One hits us and there is great loss of life, those in the states currently not being abused by Mother Nature will point a finger at us and say the same thing.

Do you really think that is how God operates?

It seems when anything bad happens – an airplane or car crashes and there is loss of life – someone asks why God would do this to them. They were good people, never said a bad word about anybody, pillars of the community.

We know enough about our earth now to know that water and air temperatures and currents bring about predictable conditions. That when the plates of the earth shift beneath us, we experience it to one degree or another.

If your neighbors home burned down because someone fell asleep and left a candle burning, would you say they deserved it? What about the kids upstairs who didn't make it out?

If nothing else in life is fair, we hope that God is.

God is not a fallible human being. God is not a human parent who responds to stimuli and makes decisions based on heartburn, fear, or anger.

Rabbi Harold Kushner was interviewed on his book, "The Lord Is My Shepherd." He wrote it in response to 9/11, when people continually asked him, "How could God let this happen?" He says, "The answer I found myself giving was that God's promise was never that life would be fair. God's promise was that when we have to confront the unfairness of life, we will be able to handle it because we won't do it alone – He'll be with us."

Bad things happen to good people.

God is with us through both the joys and tragedies of life. We are God's heart and hands when it comes to rescuing our neighbors, whether they're from our neighborhood or across an ocean. We are God's consolation, a shoulder to cry on, or an advocate to address the needs of the voiceless.

The natural workings of our planet include a variety of conditions not conducive to life of any kind. It is up to us, the literal love of God, to reach out and care for those suffering.

We don't get to read God's mind and decide if some one, some state or nation, is being judged by God in some way. We can guess, but what a burden to lay on another soul.

November 12, 2005

Be aware of Post Traumatic Stress Disorder's impact

In very real terms, we are a world led and lived in by people who are likely suffering from a condition known as Post Traumatic Stress Disorder. It is not limited to those related to the military, though it is often associated with them.

The statistics from the PTSD Alliance (www.ptsdalliance.org) are striking, and when you consider it only reflects Americans, you can see where the global picture would be mind-blowing.

The causes, signs and symptoms apply to any human, and so we're looking at a planet inhabited by perhaps a majority of children - and adults who have this "serious and common health condition."

PTSD is often defined as something that a person "has experienced, witnessed or learned about that is life-threatening or causes physical harm. It can be a single or repeated experience, causing the person to feel intense fear, horror, or a sense of helplessness." Over time, living or re-living these experiences can lead to this diagnosis.

Any thought, positive (love, joy) or negative (fear, anger), changes your body chemistry by putting hormones or chemicals, such as endorphins or cortisol, into your system. Long term exposure to "fight, flight or freeze" situations, actual or perceived, causes a myriad of mental and physical illnesses.

We can see ourselves, co-workers, and neighbors from around the globe whose day- to- day lives involve on-going terrors such as real-time or threatened physical and domestic violence, child and elder abuse, starvation, war, and natural disasters. And it's not limited to those in peril, but extends to those who observe and aid.

This could be you.

Signs of PTSD include depression, inability to focus on details, alcohol and drug abuse, asthma, chronic pain with no known medical basis such as fibromyalgia, eating disorders, and a host of other concerns.

We often seem to treat the symptom without knowing the actual cause. That is easy to do if it isn't traced back. But perhaps you see yourself or others here, know you're not alone, and that help is available.

The media has been focusing recently on what they call "compassion burn-out" or "fatigue." So much as happened to the family of humanity recently, what with the tsunami, multiple hurricanes and earthquakes; the extreme loss of life in Africa due to genocide and starvation; the "everyday" bombings somewhere in the world. We can be shell-shocked by the sheer volume of misery.

We also know we are good people who understand that we are one family, whatever our locale, faith or race, so we help our brothers and sisters whatever way we can. Whether it is physically, financially, or spiritually, we do our best to alleviate pain and suffering when it becomes known to us.

Whatever you consider to be your Source, seek its comfort, guidance and compassion. If you take better care of you, you can take better care of the children.

November 26, 2005

What did Jesus have to say about war?

Recently I listened to a sermon by Pastor Allen Cudahy from First Lutheran Community Church of Port Orchard (www.flcchurch.com) on local access television.

He said you know where your treasure is by checking your checkbook and calendar. That which is most important to you is reflected by where you put your time and money.

I did a mental review, and included my credit card statement.

In order to call something a priority or value, however, you have to have something to contrast it to. For Christians, the goal is to live a life that supports the values of Jesus of Nazareth, later known as Jesus the Christ.

Whether you call him a prophet, teacher, or savior, his life has inspired millions of souls (not just professed Christians) to live a certain way.

We are thankful for his life and all it has given to us. For some, that may be all they feel they have to give thanks for this year.

Anyone can call themselves a Christian. You can attend church, pay your tithe, read your Bible. But that's not what makes you one. It's the daily decisions, the actions taken, that define you. It's how you think, what's in your heart that makes the difference. You can do all those things that look appropriate on the surface, and still not love him. It is the true, one on one relationship with Jesus that can change your life. You don't have to consider him your savior to sit at his feet and learn.

In all my studies, I've never seen where Jesus led or condoned war. He forgave and healed. He hung out with the outcast. He challenged the government.

I am an avid watcher of NBC's "The West Wing." A couple seasons back, President Bartlett invoked the 25th amendment and Speaker of the House Glen Walken assumed the presidency.

Walken said, "Our moral values system only works if everybody plays by the same rules." Wow! That floored me. Do you believe that to be true? I've heard a form of that from real politicians who say they are Christians.

"We'd love to turn the other cheek like Jesus did, but times have changed – you have to fight fire with fire. We don't want to, but we have to kill them because they killed us or because they might try to. And we wish we didn't have to send our kids into harm's way, but it's the price of freedom."

Good people agonize and suffer because they can find no other way out of the problem.

Is war inevitable? Is Jesus' teaching now irrelevant? Can we be Christian and not follow the leader? If we want to maintain our freedom in this country, are we doomed to it if other people and countries threaten or attack us? Is war something we may have to do, even if our religious beliefs tell us not to? And that isn't limited to Christians, then. Right?

December 24, 2005

Life's trials can be an opportunity for conversion

You may recall the story of Saul of Tarsus in Acts 9, on his way to Damascus. He was going there to see if he could find any adherent's of the Way to throw into prison, when he was blinded by a light and heard a disembodied voice asking him, "Why are you persecuting me?"

"Who are you?"

"It's me, Jesus."

What follows is one of the greatest stories of conversion we have. And not from one religion to another, but a sea-change for any individual; a radical change of the heart and mind.

The others with him saw the flash of light, but did not hear the voice.

It wasn't for them. Not at that particular moment. While a conversion experience can be taken on by anyone, not everyone is in a place in themselves to do the internal housecleaning required to bring it to fruition. Not everyone sees the events and trials in their lives as an opportunity to engage it; they may just think they're going through hell. Others suffer, coming through it as a new person at the other end, not knowing what it was they experienced.

Metanoia is a Greek word meaning "new mind", "change of mind", or "beyond the mind." It's also referred to as conversion, transformation, or enlightenment.

I've never known it not to be painful. Identifying, struggling with, and releasing established ways of being and relating to the world rarely comes without struggle.

Think of it this way. A seed, in order to grow, must crack and break open in fertile soil in order for light and water to enter.

Light and water. Think about that.

You are the seed. What would it take to crack you open, and make you receptive to visceral change?

We are far more likely to come to God initially out of need than want.

When life is going good, i.e. we can pay all our bills, family is healthy, and life is absent of most conflict, we are less likely to seek God in a personal way. Unconsciously perhaps, it can turn into "I'm happy visiting with my friends and sitting in my regular pew" at a place of worship, participating on a board or committee, teaching youth or seniors – all well and good, mind you. But missing the bliss of an intimate experience with the Creator.

This could relate to the Garden of Eden in Genesis. Life was fine, they had everything they needed. They didn't want for anything. Is it only in needing that we reach for God? Perhaps initially. But there is more.

Do you want more? Do you sense, or ache, to live a life that makes "praying without ceasing" possible? Do you want a relationship with your Creator that isn't based on need, but on love? It's a "mutual admiration society."

Ask God for guidance. Maybe it's your time.